THE ACTION RESEARCH
DISSERTATION

THE ACTION RESEARCH
DISSERTATION
A Guide for Students and Faculty

Kathryn Herr
Montclair State University

Gary L. Anderson
New York University

SAGE Publications
Thousand Oaks ■ London ■ New Delhi

For information:

Sage Publications, Inc.
2455 Teller Road
Thousand Oaks, California 91320
E-mail: order@sagepub.com

Sage Publications Ltd.
1 Oliver's Yard
55 City Road
London EC1Y 1SP
United Kingdom

Sage Publications India Pvt. Ltd.
B-42, Panchsheel Enclave
Post Box 4109
New Delhi 110 017 India

Printed in the United States of America on acid-free paper.

Library of Congress Cataloging-in-Publication Data

Herr, Kathryn.
The action research dissertation: a guide for students and faculty / Kathryn Herr, Montclair State University Gary L. Anderson New York University.
    p. cm.
Includes bibliographical references and index.
ISBN 0-7619-2990-8 (cloth)—ISBN 0-7619-2991-6 (pbk.)
   1. Social sciences—Research. 2. Action research. 3. Dissertations, Academic—Authorship. 4. Academic writing. I. Anderson, Gary L., 1948- II. Title.

H62.H447 2005
300'.72—dc22

                                 2004019350

05 06 07 08 09 10 9 8 7 6 5 4 3 2 1

Acquiring Editor:	Lisa Cuevas Shaw
Editorial Assistant:	Margo Crouppen
Project Editor:	Claudia A. Hoffman
Copy Editor:	Brenda Weight
Typesetter:	C&M Digitals (P) Ltd.
Indexer:	Kathleen Paparchontis

Contents

Acknowledgments

This book is part of a larger conversation we've been having for years with friends, students, and colleagues, some only known to us through their writings. We are particularly indebted to those who have read earlier drafts of this book: Mary Brydon-Miller, Davydd J. Greenwood, Donna Podems of the African Evaluation Association, Ivor Pritchard (particularly for his reading of chapter 7), and anonymous reviewers. Others allowed us to pick their brains, offered suggestions, contacts, or access to their own work; we thank Pat Maguire and James Kelly for their particular generosity in this regard. Our biggest debt is to doctoral students we have known and worked with over the years. In allowing us to think with them about their dissertation research, they have pushed our thinking and understanding of action research. For this we are grateful. We hope this book will be of use to those doctoral students yet to come.

Foreword

Patricia Maguire

Exposure to a professor considered out of touch with the complex realities in the field has led many a university student to doubt the value of a university-based education. Questions about the relevance of universities to the communities they supposedly serve fuel both formal scholarship (for example, see Boyer, 1996; Giroux & Myrsiades, 2001; Levin & Greenwood, 2001; National Association of State Universities, 2001) and informal late-night dorm room conversations. Yet doctoral students return to the university for more. Often professionals in their own right, doctoral students come back to the university setting for a range of reasons. They may seek new knowledge, deeper understanding of complex information and issues, the challenges and rewards of shared intellectual work, updated or refined skills, fresh insights, renewed relationships and personal connections, new strategies to face old problems, alliances and relationships with other people concerned about similar issues, the hope that they can contribute to their field and make a difference in the world, and, yes, even the attainment of the credentialing that universities control.

Whatever the mix of motivations, for doctoral students, the journey through the required research component of doctoral education is particularly challenging, pushing them intellectually, philosophically, emotionally, and even financially. Doctoral students may juggle fears of their own adequacies, "Am I up to this?" with fears about the relevance of the academy, "What's the university up to?" Perhaps less talked about inside the world of doctoral studies, some university faculty members likewise struggle with fears, wanting to be good dissertation advisors and committee members, as well as people who make a difference in the world through their university work. For faculty and doctoral students alike, with personal and institutional questioning comes deep scrutiny of the particular knowledge creation process that universities control and reproduce. None of this is easy sailing. So, while the graduate research process includes thrills and accomplishments, it may also include intense questioning and near paralyzing tough spots along the way. The tough spots are almost impossible to navigate without seasoned guides and a supportive learning community. Layer on top of that the additional challenges of attempting an action research dissertation, when action research arises out of critique of the very assumptions, values, and approaches that ground traditional social science, university-based research. An action research dissertation demands innovative approaches to every aspect of the dissertation process. Indeed, it demands risk taking by both doctoral candidate and faculty. As Levin and Greenwood have noted, "Universities . . . have created a variety of conditions inimical to the practice of action research . . . " (2001, p. 103). Attempting an action research dissertation can be rough sailing in largely uncharted waters.

In a nanosecond, I can bring up memories of one of my own dissertation rough spots, even though the particular incident happened twenty years ago. Before the convenience of e-mail exchange, I traveled from Gallup, New Mexico back to Amherst, Massachusetts to review my "best draft" dissertation proposal with my doctoral committee. My committee was composed of two male professors from my home department, the Center for International Education, and an outside member, a feminist anthropology professor involved in international development research related to gender and political economy. I had taken an alternative research methods course from one committee member, David Kinsey, in which he introduced us to a range of action research approaches. So I knew he would be supportive of an action research dissertation. Having never gotten my hands on an actual action research dissertation proposal, I had agonized over the many contradictions of individually writing a proposal for a participatory action research (PAR) process. Nonetheless, with a best draft dissertation proposal in hand, I faced my committee. I had counted the feminist anthropologist as an action research ally, although why I'm not sure. So I was blindsided when she tore my proposal to shreds. Throwing the proposal on the table for added effect, she dismissed months of work with the declaration, "If you want to do research, do research; if you want to organize, then go do activist work." How could I have been so stupid, her words implied, as to think that I could combine action and research in the dissertation process?

Maintaining what dignity I could, I left the meeting and sequestered myself in a stall in the women's bathroom on the third floor of Hills House South and sobbed and fumed in private. Indeed, how could I have been so stupid? How in the world could I write a proposal for an action research dissertation and then get it through the university system, with first my committee and then the institutional review board looming in the background? Where and how could I gather more allies and find guidelines for doing an action research dissertation, starting with the proposal? What were the challenges and contradictions that I would have to sort through as I struggled to work with others to generate usable knowledge through a collaborative process that just might contribute to social justice or change? And how to answer that nagging internal voice that floated the question, Is any of this even possible in the academy?

Twenty years later, it's a joy to read Kathryn Herr and Gary Anderson's book designed to help doctoral student researchers tackle these issues head on. No more being forced to comb through appendices, prefaces, endnotes, and other notes at the margins to figure out how to tackle an action research dissertation. Drawing from years of collaboration with their own graduate students and other school-based action researchers, Kathryn and Gary lay out the issues and decisions that doctoral students and their committees have to negotiate as they engage in an action research dissertation.

This volume comes out of the work that Gary and Kathryn have done for years to pry open spaces in universities for action research, to question the status quo of doctoral research, and to proactively support a potentially transformative alternative. The authors have been doing what they support doctoral students doing, that is, changing their own work environment through studying their practices as doctoral committee members, university faculty, and school-based action researchers.

In this volume, doctoral researchers are asked to sort through their own multiple positions and identities, and those of collaborators. The difficult but necessary choice points of potentially transformative knowledge creation are mapped out and named for what they are: political decisions with power dimensions that the doctoral researcher must work through and publicly articulate. Clearly, knowledge production is not a value-free or neutral endeavor. Doctoral students have to figure out which action research traditions best mesh with their own beliefs, values, commitments to social change, and organizational workplace. These are not neat, individualized academic exercises with correct answers, but messy work best done in collaboration, reflection, and conversation. New insights and knowledge are arrived at through action and research done in relationship with others.

This volume is a long-awaited and desperately needed contribution to the action research–university partnership. It's valuable for doctoral students hoping to collaborate with faculty members, other doctoral students, and community- or school-based partners on a different way of doing doctoral research and a socially engaged way of being a researcher. It's also valuable for dissertation committee members, whether experienced or novice at supporting doctoral students engaging in action research dissertations.

In many ways, the volume may be threatening to those who have resisted any alternative to traditional positivist dissertations or have somehow sidestepped discussion about the supposed objective knowledge creation process reproduced in universities. This volume gets to the heart of action research, foregrounding power relations and what those relations mean for all aspects of knowledge production. Gary and Kathryn's volume will also serve to amplify conversations about the relevancy of universities and the dissertation process and products to the pressing social and justice issues of the 21st century. It puts a wedge further in that crack in the positivist door, holding open the space for continued scrutiny of the purposes, processes, and products of research.

—*Patricia Maguire*
Gallup, New Mexico
July 2004

Boyer, E. (1996). The scholarship of engagement. *Journal of Public Service & Outreach, 1*(1).

Giroux, H., & Myrsiades, K. (Eds.). (2001). *Beyond the corporate university.* Lanham, ND: Rowman & Littlefield.

Levin, M., & Greenwood, D. (2001). Pragmatic action research and the struggle to transform universities into learning communities. In P. Reason & H. Bradbury (Eds.), *Handbook of action research* (pp. 103–113). London: Sage.

National Association of State Universities and Land-Grant Colleges. (2001). Returning to our roots: Executive summaries of the reports of the Kellogg Commission on the future of state and land-grant universities. Washington, DC.

Preface

L ike many university professors before us, we wrote this book because we couldn't find one that addressed our instructional needs. We found that many graduate students were struggling with turning action research projects into master's theses or doctoral dissertations and had little guidance in this effort. Some were not even our students, but were struggling with dissertation committees that simply were not trained to understand the complexities of this type of research. Both of us have chaired action research dissertations, and coauthor Herr has engaged extensively in action research herself with middle and high school students and faculty (Herr, 1995, 1999a, 1999b, 1999c, 1999d). Most applied fields and professional schools in universities offer Ph.D.s as well as more explicitly applied doctorate and master's degrees. Nevertheless, most fields have not thought through the issues of organizational or community insiders doing research in their own settings or outsiders doing research that views insiders as full participants rather than as research subjects or informants.

Traditional positivist or naturalist paradigms do not capture the unique dilemmas faced by action researchers. Many excellent books exist that are guides to action research in general. In fact, we published one ourselves a decade ago (Anderson, Herr, & Nihlen, 1994). These books, however, fail to address the specific issues that arise in turning an action research project into a dissertation. For instance, a major goal of action research is to generate local knowledge that is fed back into the setting. However, dissertations demand public knowledge that is transferable to other settings and written up in such a way that others can see its application to their settings.

While we will focus on how action research requires a somewhat unique approach to writing the dissertation, we will not provide an introduction to action research itself because many excellent introductions exist from various perspectives. An excellent overview is Greenwood and Levin (1998). Some introductory books provide step-by-step approaches, while others provide a more descriptive approach, drawing on examples. Introductions have appeared in various disciplines such as public health (Minkler & Wallerstein, 2002;

Morton-Cooper, 2000; Stringer & Genat, 2004), social work (Fuller & Petch, 1995), organizational studies (McNiff & Whitehead, 2000); education (Anderson, Herr, & Nihlen, 1994; Cochran-Smith & Lytle, 1993; Hubbard & Power, 1999; Mills, 2002); community development (Jason et al., 2003); and counseling (McLeod, 1999).

Action research is often collaborative, whereas the culture of dissertations demands individual demonstration of competence. Because of its emergent design and cyclical revision of research questions, an action research dissertation requires unique decisions about how to write a proposal, how to structure the dissertation itself, how to narrate the "findings," and how to defend the final product. In fact, it is often difficult to think of action research as a linear product with a finite ending, as successful projects can spiral on for years. For many students, the biggest problem is either locating dissertation committee members who understand this type of research or legitimating it to committee members who may be open-minded but unfamiliar with the methodology. In this sense, the book is written for both doctoral students and their dissertation committees.

We also hope to provide a book that brings the interests of distinct action research communities together. In spite of claims to being interdisciplinary, action researchers tend to work within their own disciplinary boundaries. Pick up a book or an article by an action researcher in education and there are few citations outside the field. The same is true for those who use action research for organizational development, international development, social work or health fields. Coauthor Herr has a master's and a Ph.D. in social work but has done most of her action research in schools; coauthor Anderson is an educator and has written primarily about education. Therefore, while our expertise is primarily in education action research, we have worked hard to be as inclusive of other fields as possible.

Most doctoral students are formally trained in quantitative and qualitative research methods and seldom encounter an action research course. Increasingly, action research courses are appearing in graduate programs, and it is receiving its own chapter in some introductory research texts (see Gall, Gall, & Borg, 2003). Because most doctoral students have some notion of what a traditional dissertation looks like, we do not attempt to reproduce the kind of step-by-step guide provided by how-to books on dissertations. We do not oppose such books; many are excellent and we suggest students read these manuals alongside this book (see Glatthorm, 1998; Hepner & Hepner, 2003; Meloy, 2001; Piantanida & Garman, 1999; Rudestam & Newton, 1992). In this book, we are more interested in helping students understand the ways action research dissertations are different from more traditional dissertations and to prepare students and their committees for the unique dilemmas that action research raises around validity, positionality, design, write-up, ethics, and defense of the dissertation.

We believe that the best way to prepare to write an action research dissertation is to read action research dissertations. It is remarkable that doctoral students are seldom assigned dissertations to read in doctoral seminars. For this reason, we often refer readers to dissertations that might serve as exemplars. To avoid an excessively didactic approach, we also try to provide brief examples from action research dissertations of how various students have dealt with issues of epistemology, methodology, ethics, validity, narration, and so on. Because action research dissertations do not follow a step-by-step chronological order, we have not taken this linear approach. We believe that as students understand the unique dilemmas of writing up an action research dissertation, they can employ the very cycles of plan-act-observe-reflect to their own emerging document.

Although the book represents mostly original work, we have incorporated and updated some previous work. Sections of chapter 2 on the history of action research are updated from chapter 2 of Anderson, Herr, and Nihlen (1994). Some of the work on positionality in chapter 3 is updated from Anderson and Jones (2000). The section on validity criteria in chapter 4 is updated from Anderson and Herr (1999).

The order of chapters is somewhat arbitrary; they can be read in any order. We see the book as a resource book, and certain chapters may become more relevant at different stages in the dissertation process. Graduate students who want a neat, step-by-step approach to research should not choose action research for a dissertation. For instance, a traditional five-chapter survey research dissertation using inferential statistics to analyze data is less labor intensive and can be done without leaving one's office. Unlike traditional dissertations that insist on a dispassionate, distanced attitude toward one's research, action research is often chosen by doctoral students because they are passionate about their topic, their setting, and coparticipants. We have attempted to capture this passionate tone, while providing a balanced and useful guide to carving a dissertation out of the exciting but always messy process of action research.

1

Introduction

What is an Action Research Dissertation?

Dissertations in the social sciences are not what they used to be. Before the advent of more qualitative and action-oriented research, advice on how to do the standard five-chapter dissertation was fairly clear. Students were advised to begin in linear fashion, producing the first three chapters for the proposal defense and then adding a chapter to report findings and another for implications and recommendations after the data were gathered and analyzed. The qualitative dissertation, with its more emergent design and narrative style, challenged the notion that three completed chapters could be defended as a proposal or that five chapters were enough to effectively "display" qualitative data. Over the past 30 years, dissertation committees and Institutional Review Boards (IRBs) have become more tolerant of the unique needs of qualitative researchers.

The action research dissertation is the new kid on the block, and it is coming under intense scrutiny by both dissertation committees and IRBs. While action research shares some similarities with qualitative research (and even quantitative research), it is different in that research participants themselves are either in control of the research or are participants in the design and methodology of the research. Committee members and IRBs are often stymied by the cyclical nature of action research as well as its purposes, which transcend mere knowledge generation to include personal and professional growth and organizational and community empowerment. IRBs are confused about risk factors in settings in which research subjects are participants in the research at the same time that they are, often, subordinates within the organizational settings. These power relations are further complicated when the action researcher is also an insider to the organization. Furthermore, action research often uses a narrative style that allows the researcher to reflect on the research

1

process as well as the findings, which seldom can be easily formulated as propositional knowledge. Finally, action research has grown out of very different research traditions and has manifested itself differently in different disciplines and fields of study. In fact, action research is inherently interdisciplinary and seldom fits neatly into the norms of a particular discipline or field.

Historically, action researchers were academics or professional researchers who involved research participants in their studies to a greater extent than was typical with traditional research. In fact, some social scientists argue that participatory forms of action research are merely variants of applied research and that its difference consists merely of the degree to which participants are included (Spjelkavik, 1999). In some cases, participants are involved from the inception of the research to the writing and presentation of the final report. Increasing numbers of doctoral students in fields such as community psychology, social work, nursing, and international development want to do dissertation studies in which their outsider status is tempered by collaboration with insiders, and in which action is central to the research. Many action research dissertations that we will discuss in this book are of this type. However, as more working professionals have begun receiving doctoral degrees, there has been a tendency for action researchers to be insiders to their professional settings, making them at once both researcher and practitioner. This is particularly true of Ed.D. (doctorate in education) programs, which have produced a significant number of dissertation studies in recent years done by organizational insiders. These practitioner researchers often want to study their own contexts because they want the research to make a difference in their own setting and sometimes, often mistakenly, because they think it will be more convenient and easier to do the study where they work.

The Many Faces of Action Research

So what is action research? Perhaps its most important feature is that it shifts its locus of control in varying degrees from professional or academic researchers to those who have been traditionally called the subjects of research. There are several terms in current use that describe research done either by or in collaboration with practitioners and/or community members. The most common ones are *action research; participatory action research (PAR); practitioner research; action science; collaborative action research; cooperative inquiry; educative research; appreciative inquiry; emancipatory praxis; community-based participatory research; teacher research; participatory rural appraisal; feminist action research; feminist, antiracist participatory action research; and advocacy activist, or militant research.* As we will make clear in chapter 2, each of these terms connotes different purposes, positionalities, espistemologies, ideological commitments, and, in many cases, different research traditions that grew out of very different social contexts.

We have chosen to use the term *action research* for this book for pragmatic and philosophical reasons. Pragmatically, it is probably the most generically used term in all disciplines and fields of study, so it serves as an umbrella term for the others. It also makes *action* central to the research enterprise and sets up nicely a tension with traditional research, which tends to take a more distanced approach to research settings. Much like those who study natural experiments, action researchers tend to study ongoing actions that are taken in a setting. Such action-oriented research would raise issues of reactivity for traditional researchers, both qualitative and quantitative. Traditional researchers see their impact on the setting either as positive (as using carefully planned and controlled treatments in an experimental design) or as negative (as contaminating or distorting ongoing events in a natural setting).

In some fields, such as education, nursing, and social work, the term *practitioner research* (or, more specifically, *teacher research, administrator research,* etc.) has gained popularity (particularly in the U.S.). This term implies that insiders to the setting are the researchers, whereas in other traditions of action research, the researcher is an outsider who collaborates to varying degrees with insider practitioners or community members. The term *action research* leaves the positionality (insider or outsider) of the researcher open. The term *practitioner researcher* places the insider/practitioner at the center of the research, but often tends to decenter other important stakeholders, such as clients and other community members. Because of this, many argue that action research should always be collaborative regardless of whether the researcher is an outsider or insider to the setting under study. We will return repeatedly to this issue of positionality throughout the book, because how action researchers position themselves vis-à-vis the setting under study will determine how one thinks about power relations, research ethics, and the validity or trustworthiness of the study's findings.

Toward a Definition of Action Research

Although the plethora of terms coined to describe this research reflects wide disagreement on many key issues, most agree on the following: action research is inquiry that is done *by* or *with* insiders to an organization or community, but never *to* or *on* them. It is a reflective process, but is different from isolated, spontaneous reflection in that it is deliberately and systematically undertaken and generally requires that some form of evidence be presented to support assertions. What constitutes evidence or, in more traditional terms, data is still being debated. Action research is oriented to some action or cycle of actions that organizational or community members have taken, are taking, or wish to take to address a particular problematic situation. The idea is that changes occur either within the setting and/or within the researchers themselves.

Action research is best done in collaboration with others who have a stake in the problem under investigation. Collaboration for insiders involves outsiders with relevant skills or resources (e.g., dissertation committees, methodology consultants), though most agree that the perceived need for change should come from within the setting. Even in a case in which a lone practitioner is studying his or her own practice, participation or at least ongoing feedback should be sought from other stakeholders in the setting or community in order to ensure a democratic outcome and provide an alternative source of explanations. The issue of collaboration and participation creates important tensions in the case of action research dissertations, because the culture of dissertations discourages collaborative work.

Like all forms of inquiry, action research is *value-laden*. Although most practitioners or communities hope that action research will solve pressing problems or improve their practice, what constitutes improvement or a solution is not self-evident. It is particularly problematic in fields that do not have consensus on basic aims. Action research takes place in settings that reflect a society characterized by conflicting values and an unequal distribution of resources and power. Here the notion of reflexivity is crucial because action researchers must interrogate received notions of improvement or solutions in terms of who ultimately benefits from the actions undertaken.

Several more concise definitions exist in the growing body of literature on action research. For example, McKernan (1988) described it as "a form of self-reflective problem solving, which enables practitioners to better understand and solve pressing problems in social settings" (p. 6). McCutcheon and Jung (1990) agree but add an emphasis on collaboration:

> systematic inquiry that is collective, collaborative, self-reflective, critical, and undertaken by the participants of the inquiry. The goals of such research are the understanding of practice and the articulation of a rationale or philosophy of practice in order to improve practice. (p. 148)

Kemmis and McTaggart (1987), writing about education, add the goal of social justice to their definition:

> a form of *collective*, self-reflective enquiry undertaken by participants in social situations in order to improve the rationality and justice of their own social or educational practices, as well as their understanding of these practices and the situations in which these practices are carried out. Groups of participants can be teachers, students, principals, parents, and other community members—any group with a shared concern. The approach is only Action Research when it is *collaborative*, though it is important to realize that the Action Research of the group

is achieved through the *critically examined action* of the individual group members. (p. 6)

Argyris and Schon (1991), who focus on organizational and professional development, describe the goals and methods of the action research tradition.

Action Research takes its cues—its questions, puzzles, and problems—from the perceptions of practitioners within particular, local practice contexts. It bounds episodes of research according to the boundaries of the local context. It builds descriptions and theories within the practice context itself, and tests them there through *intervention experiments*—that is, through experiments that bear the double burden of testing hypotheses and effecting some (putatively) desired change in the situation. (p. 86)

The double burden that the authors refer to is the concern with both action (improvement of practice, social change, and the like) and research (creating valid knowledge about practice) and, according to the authors, this sets up a conflict between the rigor and the relevance of the research—a conflict that has been viewed as both an advantage and disadvantage by different commentators. Unlike traditional social science research that frowns on intervening in any way in the research setting, action research demands some form of intervention. For the action researcher, these interventions constitute a spiral of action cycles in which one undertakes

1. to develop a *plan* of action to improve what is already happening;

2. to *act* to implement the plan;

3. to *observe* the effects of action in the context in which it occurs;

4. to *reflect* on these effects as a basis for further planning, subsequent action and on, through a succession of cycles. (Kemmis, 1982, p. 7)

This cycle of activities forms an action research spiral in which each cycle increases the researchers' knowledge of the original question, puzzle, or problem and, it is hoped, leads to its solution.

We prefer to remain as eclectic as possible with regard to a definition of action research; however, the definition that a researcher chooses should be made clear in a dissertation. This definition will then determine the kinds of epistemological, ethical, and political decisions a researcher will have to make throughout the dissertation study. Furthermore, we recommend that researchers make this decision-making process explicit in the dissertation itself, either in the body or in an appendix. Until action research is as well understood as traditional methodologies, such discussions may be needed to reassure (and educate) skeptical dissertation committee members.

The Action Research Dissertation

Unfortunately, there is more writing *about* action research than documentation of actual research studies. This is, in part, because those who engage in action research projects are often more interested in generating knowledge that can be fed back into the setting under study than generating knowledge that can be shared beyond the setting. Drawing on Geertz's (1983) work on "local knowledge" in anthropology, Cochran-Smith and Lytle (1993) make a distinction between the generation of local and public knowledge in action research. With reference to teachers, they use the term *local knowledge* "to signal both what teachers come to know about their own knowledge through teacher research and what communities of teacher researchers come to know when they build knowledge collaboratively" (p. 45). Thus, local knowledge is most often shared, if at all, with only an immediate community of practitioners or community members. It is meant to address the immediate needs of people in specific settings, and it is this utility of knowledge generated by action research that represents one of its major strengths.

The dissertation represents scholarship that generally makes knowledge claims that are generalizable, or transferable, beyond the immediate setting. This means that an action research study for a dissertation must consider how the knowledge generated can be utilized by those in the setting, as well as by those beyond the setting. This can be done in a number of ways. A dissertation may represent the documentation of a successful collaboration and be used as a case study of not only the process but also the product of the collaboration. This becomes public knowledge to the extent that the knowledge is transferred to someone in a receiving context that is similar (i.e., another battered women's shelter, another science classroom, another community, etc.) to the sending context that produced the study. Qualitative and case study researchers refer to this as the external validity, or *transferability,* of the findings.

Another way that knowledge is transferable is when dissertations generate new theory that can be used to help explain similar problems in other contexts. Anderson, Herr, and Nihlen (1994) describe an action research study by classroom teacher Cynthia Ballenger (1992; see also Ballenger, 1998) that informed and expanded the existing theory base in early childhood literacy. She documented what she eventually called the "shadow curriculum," a product of children's social networks in the classroom that supplements the enacted curriculum.

Action research can also result in products and instruments that can be used in other settings. Lynne Mock (1999), whose dissertation is discussed in chapter 5, developed and validated the Personal Vision Scale to explore the concept of transformational leadership in a community setting. This scale, which assesses various stages in the leader's visioning process, can be used by other community groups in selecting and training community leaders.

Action research dissertations represent an important source of documentation of action research studies as well as knowledge about various social practices. The recent growth of doctorate in education (Ed.D.) programs and programs for applied doctoral degrees in fields such as social work, nursing, and criminology have provided an important space for action research dissertations. Unfortunately, few academic faculty are trained in action research—even in applied fields—and thus lack the skills to guide students through the complex and messy process of action research. Ironically, many of the students in applied doctoral programs are working full time in organizations and communities while enrolled at the university. It is hard to imagine a better scenario for fostering action research, and yet few applied doctorate programs teach action research methods and even fewer Ph.D. programs do (see Anderson, 2002; Anderson & Herr, 1999, for a further discussion of this problem). Nevertheless, the number of action research courses in professional schools and applied fields appears to be growing. We hope this book will help both faculty and students think through the complex dilemmas that action research presents for master's theses and doctoral dissertations, as well as its wider dissemination through publication.

2

Action Research Traditions and Knowledge Interests

As we discussed in chapter 1, action research is a cover term for several approaches that have emerged from different traditions. Everyone who uses action research for a dissertation should be steeped in the particular tradition they are working out of and the attendant methodological, epistemological, and political dilemmas. We do not pretend to provide this level of grounding in this chapter, but we do try to provide some sense of how these traditions relate to each other and where students and faculty can go for more extensive accounts. There are several historical overviews of action research, but most are told from a particular intellectual and social tradition, such as the overviews provided by Anderson, Herr, and Nihlen (1994, practitioner research); Argyris, Putnam, and Smith (1985, action science); Bullough and Pinnegar (2001, self-study); Chambers (1997, participatory rural appraisal); Cochran-Smith and Lytle (1993, teacher research); Fals Borda (2002, participatory action research); Greenwood and Levin (1998, action research); and Maguire (1987, feminist participatory action research). In this section, we will try to be as inclusive as possible so that students consulting this book for guidance on their dissertations can find their particular tradition of action research represented. There is also a need for a participatory dialogue among these traditions, which academic departmentalization has tended to balkanize into self-contained scholarly communities.

Historians are in the business of creating—not discovering or interpreting—historical meaning. In this chapter, we have done our best to get our "facts" straight, but the meaning one makes of them will depend on who is telling the story. To our knowledge, no attempt at a comprehensive history of action research exists, and our intent is not to provide it here. While the previous chapter attempted to provide some common elements of action research, there may be as much variation across action research traditions as there is between action research and some mainstream approaches to research. Some action research is group oriented and some is individual oriented; some is done by those within the setting and some is done by change agents from outside the organization in collaboration with insiders; and some is highly participatory and some is much less so. Similarly, some see the goal of action research as *improving* practice or *developing* individuals, whereas others see its goal as *transforming* practice and participants. Debates rage within action research around these issues.

To the extent possible, our goal in this book is to present all of these perspectives in an evenhanded way. We believe that action researchers who write dissertations should be able to defend the particular tradition from which they have chosen to work, as well as to appreciate—and not naively conflate—differences among traditions. In many cases, the issue is not that one or another tradition is better, but that it may be more or less appropriate to the context of a particular study. Or, students may find one approach to action research more congruent with their own set of beliefs, values, and goals.

The popularity of action research has waxed and waned during the second half of the twentieth century. Ironically, its popularity has often been linked to trends in areas as disparate as business administration and anticapitalist, grassroots movements. We caution students not to ignore differences or transfer models inappropriately beyond the contexts for which they were developed. While a revolutionary thinker like Paulo Freire and a business guru like W.E. Deming may both have advocated a cycle of inquiry involving *plan-act-observe-reflect,* this does not mean that their two philosophies are epistemologically, methodologically, or ideologically compatible. In the public sector, there has been a growing—but, in our opinion, misguided—influence of business models and techniques designed to increase productivity and accountability. Perhaps the most pervasive are the techniques associated with total quality management that incorporate cycles of plan-act-observe-reflect and methods of statistical control that carry the assumptions of the business models from which they were derived. Using statistical control to eliminate variation in a product makes perfect sense when mass-producing hamburgers or jet engines. However, it makes much less sense for healing patients, educating children, or solving community problems.

On the end of the continuum farthest from business-oriented versions is action research as emancipatory practice aimed at helping an oppressed group to identify and act on social policies and practices that keep unequal power relations in place. Here action research is working with an oppressed community to identify what Freire (1970) called *generative themes,* or issues that the community agreed had highest priority. In this way, action research is seen as challenging traditional notions of change and change agency that bring in outside experts to solve local problems. Participatory action research (PAR) tempers this expert knowledge with the expertise of locals about their own problems and solutions.

As discussed in the introduction, action researchers are often more interested in their projects than in writing them up. Practitioners are too immersed in their day-to-day work, and consultants tend to move from project deadline to project deadline. Neither have the leisure of those who work in the academy to write up research reports. This is one reason why action research dissertations are such a potentially important contribution to a field's knowledge base. Action research dissertations contain a local perspective that few traditional researchers are able to provide. A dissertation forces action researchers to think not only about what knowledge they have generated that can be fed back into the setting (local knowledge), but also what knowledge they have generated that is transferable to other settings (public knowledge). As more action research dissertations are written, it is hoped that more of them will find their way into publication. For now, however, dissertation abstracts are an important source of action research studies.[1] Although only some are the product of dissertations, excellent sources for book-length published action research include the *Dialogues on Work and Innovation* series at John Benjamins Publishing Company and the *Practitioner Research* series at Teachers College Press.[2]

The Multiple Traditions of Action Research

Action research is carried out under diverse intellectual traditions, and these traditions are distinct from and generally at odds with the mainstream academic research traditions in the social sciences. It may be helpful to think of these traditions as distinct scientific communities that are in constant evolution. The notion of scientific community is important because what "counts" as valid research is what sociologists call a *social construction* (Berger & Luckmann, 1967). At different times, in different social contexts, what constitutes valid ways of creating knowledge will vary. It is not by accident, for example, that emancipatory, grassroots approaches to research emerged from the oppressive social conditions of the third world and among disenfranchised groups in the U.S. It is also not surprising from a historical perspective that positivistic, quantitative methods—what Mills (1959) called *abstracted empiricism*—emerged as dominant in the social sciences in the U.S. during the mid-twentieth century when social engineering was a popular approach to social problem solving.

In this chapter, we provide a highly condensed account of a variety of action research traditions. There is only space to whet the reader's appetite to further explore the work summarized here. We invite the reader to delve into those traditions that are of particular interest. We hope that researchers and practitioners, armed with knowledge of previous attempts to promote action research, will be in a better position to articulate the importance and legitimacy of their own work.

Action Research and Organizational Development/Learning

Some view the origins of action research as being in the work of Kurt Lewin and the group-dynamics movement of the 1940s. Although Lewin was not the first to use or advocate action research, he was the first to develop a theory of action research that made it a respectable form of research in the social sciences. Lewin believed that knowledge should be created from problem solving in real-life situations. Among the problems he studied were those related to production in factories and discrimination against minority groups (Lewin, 1946, 1948). His work on human dynamics in groups evolved into later research on work teams and site-based management, and his theories of organizational and social change were taken up by a growing human relations and organizational development movement. Using a thermodynamic metaphor of unfreezing, floating, and freezing matter, he saw change as a series of discrete episodes. This view of change was later criticized by Argyris and Schon (1974), who argued that it limited change to short-term interventions that move from one stable state to another rather than encouraging continuous organizational learning that could be sustained over time.

Current business models promote work teams, statistical control, continuous improvement, site-based management, and so forth, for both private and public sector organizations. While many practitioners believe these are recent innovations, they in fact go back to the early work of Lewin and the growing critique of industries' dependence on the Taylorist principles of hierarchy, bureaucracy, direct supervision, and other mechanistic forms of worker control. Until the 1940s, it was believed by most industrialists that workers could be manipulated in much the same way that machinery was manipulated. Time and motion studies, inspired by Frederick Taylor, were done in workplaces to determine which work variables to manipulate in order to raise worker productivity.

By the 1940s, the human relations movement's critique of Taylorism was widely known and many industrialists were experimenting with these more worker-centered, participatory techniques. The human relations movement was associated with the well-known Hawthorne studies and theorists such as Elton Mayo and George Homans and, somewhat later, Kurt Lewin. During the late 1950s and 1960s, the human relations movement evolved into the human resources school associated with Douglas McGregor and Frederick Herzberg. Most of the assumptions of these theorists concerning human motivation and, later, human capital theory are still very much a part of management and organizational theory. Action research's insistence on worker participation played an important role in these movements but was often used as a management technique to get worker buy-in. However, it also had the potential to democratize workplaces and heed Lewin's call for theory grounded in local problem solving. (For a critique of this movement, see Carey, 1997.)

Lewin's action research was taken up in the U.S. by external consultants who set up controlled experiments and measured results. This tradition of action research was captured for over 40 years by a positivist approach that manipulated isolated variables. Levin (1999) speculates on why this trend occurred in the U.S.

> First, the strong professional norms within American academia allowed little freedom to break out of the barriers defined by positivistic social science. Second, mainstream action research in the U.S. was linked to businesses competing in the marketplace. It was generally contracted and paid for by companies. In this context, action research soon became organizational development work in which the core interest was organizational change in support of a power elite's interests. The research part was subordinated to other goals and the open-ended inquiry dimension disappeared. (p. 26)

Europe and the third world, then, were more fertile ground for the development of action research, particularly in its participatory forms. In Europe, where there was strong labor union participation, the tendency for management control of the process was somewhat lessened, and social movements in the third world, particularly in Latin America, embraced action research as a form of activist or militant research.

Perhaps one of the most ambitious action research projects in workplace democracy was the study of the Mondragon cooperatives in the Basque region of Spain. Led by Davydd Greenwood, it represents in many ways a classic case study of PAR in which insiders and outsiders to the setting set a research agenda together and collaborate on all phases of the research. The Mondragon cooperatives are a large group of labor-managed businesses in Spain that became an international model for workplace democracy. Much previous experimentation in workplace democracy, such as the projects undertaken in the Tavistock Institute of Human Relations in London or the Industrial Democracy Project in Norway, ultimately lost their emphasis on the democratic participation of workers (Greenwood & Levin, 1998). This was particularly true in the U.S., where the human relations movement was viewed by many as a wedge against unionism (Carey, 1997). Thus, the Mondragon experiment attracted many advocates of worker participation because the experiment involved not only workplace democracy but also worker control of the business itself.

The Mondragon action research project began when William Foote White was invited to Mondragon to help them solve problems he had identified in a previous research visit. He elicited the aid of Cornell colleague and anthropologist Davydd Greenwood, who had done fieldwork in the Basque region where Mondragon is located. The work teams that Greenwood encountered were expecting a set of lectures from an expert on organizational culture. To their surprise, Greenwood insisted that the Mondragon workers become involved in the project as participants, helping to identify problems and research questions. Thus began a 3-year participatory research project that has been extensively documented in terms of both the obstacles that were encountered in creating a participatory research team and the findings that resulted from the study (Gonzalez, 1991; Greenwood & Gonzalez, 1992; Greenwood & Levin, 1998). The documentation is of particular interest because the director of personnel of the Fagor Group at Mondragon, Jose Luis Gonzalez, and the Cornell researcher, Davydd Greenwood, have both published extensively on both the process and findings of the study.

Action research in the tradition of organizational development and workplace democracy has more recently taken what van Beinum (1999) calls a communicative turn, influenced primarily by a group of Scandinavian-based researchers working out of a long tradition of workplace democracy. From 1985–1990, a state-funded Swedish research program, Leadership, Organization and Codetermination, funded several landmark action research studies. After funding ended in 1990, the Scandinavian-based Action Research Development Program (ACRES) was formed as a collaboration between the Swedish Center for Working Life and the Norwegian University of Science and Technology in Trondheim, Norway.

Drawing on the work of Habermas, Wittgenstein, and Vygotsky and postmodern theories of language and discourse, researchers associated with this movement view democratic organizational development as closely linked to language and communication. Drawing on Habermas, they view organizational life as an "internal public sphere" in much the same way that Habermas theorized communication in a broader public sphere.[3] Not surprisingly, a central concept within this approach is *dialogue*, and a variety of forums have been developed in which dialogue is encouraged and guided. This perspective has been described in detail in several publications (Engelstad & Gustavsen, 1993; Gustavsen, 1992; Palshaugen, 1998), so we will not describe it in detail here. Palshaugen's (1998) *The End of Organizational Theory?* describes an action research study that was an attempt at organization development through the reorganization of discourses.

Action Science

Action science is largely associated with the work of Chris Argyris (Argyris et al., 1985), whose central concern is the ability of organizations to learn.

Based on the notion of organizations as self-correcting systems, he, like the Scandinavian researchers, sees communication as central to organizational change. He and his associates have also incorporated aspects of critical theory into their work, particularly Habermas (1979), whose theory of communication seeks to establish nondistorted communication in which the force of the better argument prevails, as judged in free and open discussion.

Argyris also wishes to return to action research its scientific dimension, arguing that the problem-solving focus of action research has moved it too far away from the tasks of theory building and testing. The goal of an action science, according to Argyris et al. (1985), is the generation of "knowledge that is useful, valid, descriptive of the world, and informative of how we might change it" (p. x). Argyris has also criticized some types of action research for adhering to traditional social science notions of "rigorous research," arguing that "to attain a certain level of rigor, the methodology may become so disconnected from the reality it is designed to understand that it is no longer useful" (p. x).

Drawing on the previous work of Dewey and Lewin and often writing with Donald Schon (Argyris & Schon, 1974), Argyris over the years has evolved an intervention strategy for changing the status quo that stresses organizational learning. According to Argyris et al. (1985),

> In social life, the status quo exists because the norms and rules learned through socialization have been internalized and are continually reinforced. Human beings learn which skills work within the status quo and which do not work. The more the skills work, the more they influence individuals' sense of competence. Individuals draw on such skills and justify their use by identifying the values embedded in them and adhering to these values. The interdependence among norms, rules, skills, and values creates a pattern called the status quo that becomes so omnipresent as to be taken for granted and to go unchallenged. Precisely because these patterns are taken for granted, precisely because these skills are automatic, precisely because values are internalized, the status quo and individuals' personal responsibility for maintaining it cannot be studied without confronting it. (p. xi)

Argyris's work is important for action researchers because it suggests why many institutions may not be thrilled at the idea of close examination. It is also important because, unless solutions to the problems under study tap into the complex theories of action that underlie and maintain the status quo, problems will only be solved in a superficial and temporary manner.

Robinson (1993), a former student of Argyris, describes the need for problem-based methodology in educational research:

> Much research has failed to influence educational problems because it has separated problematic practices from the pre-theorized problem-solving processes that gave rise to them and which render them sensible to those who engage in

them. Once practice is understood in this way, the theorizing and reasoning of practitioners becomes a key to understanding what sustains problematic practice. Problem-based methodology provides a way of uncovering, evaluating and, if necessary, reconstructing these theories of action. (p. 256)

What Robinson's work implies is that practitioner research should not simply promote practitioners' "practical theories" (Sanders & McCutcheon, 1986) in a nonproblematic way, but rather explore in self-reflective ways how some practical theories may be perpetuating the very problems practitioners identify for study.

Participatory Research: The Legacy of Paulo Freire

The work of Miles Horton and John Gaventa of the Highlander Center served as an early inspiration for participatory research in North America (Gaventa & Horton, 1981; Lewis, 2002), but it was the appearance of Paulo Freire's *Pedagogy of the Oppressed* in English in 1970 that galvanized critical researchers in the U.S. Long before feminists and critical theorists began their critique of politically conservative and white, male-dominated action research models, a model of action research as liberation was taking hold in Latin America. After the Brazilian military coup of 1964, Paulo Freire went into exile in Chile. During the late 1960s and early 1970s, Freire and a group of Chilean literacy educators began a series of *thematic research* projects. Freire (1970) views thematic research as a highly inductive process in which research is seen as a form of social action. In this type of research, *generative themes,* or issues of vital importance to community members, are identified and used as a basis for literacy instruction and also studied in a collaborative fashion. Such projects have a dual purpose: (a) to help participants (usually adults) acquire literacy and (b) to help them engage in social critique and social action. In other words, literacy involves learning to read the word and the world.

In 1976, the Participatory Research Group was created by the International Council of Adult Education in Toronto and its network centers around the world. During the last three decades, participatory research has been done all over Latin America and the rest of the third world (Brown & Tandon, 1983; Fals Borda, 2002; Gaventa, 1988; Hall, 2002; Yopo, 1984). The first World Symposium of Action Research was held in Cartagena, Colombia in 1977. This conference has since been held throughout the world and attracts thousands of attendees (Wallerstein & Duran, 2003).

Although methodological considerations depend on the context within which the study is undertaken, de Schutter and Yopo (1981) describe the following as general characteristics of participatory research:

- The point of departure for participatory research is a vision of social events as contextualized by macro-level social forces;
- Social processes and structures are understood within a historical context;
- Theory and practice are integrated;
- The subject-object relationship is transformed into a subject-subject relationship through dialogue;
- Research and action (including education itself) become a single process;
- The community and researcher together produce critical knowledge aimed at social transformation;
- The results of research are immediately applied to a concrete situation. (p. 68)

In Freirean-inspired participatory research, the academic research model is challenged at almost every point. The dualisms of macro/micro, theory/practice, subject/object, and research/ teaching are collapsed. This perspective also challenges many of the premises of more traditional models of action research. Many of the criticisms are similar to the feminist critique of action research discussed below. Brown and Tandon (1983) indicate that traditional action research tends to concentrate on an individual or group level of analysis of problems, whereas participatory research, with its more emancipatory emphasis, tends to focus on a broader societal analysis. Traditional action research tends to emphasize issues of efficiency and improvement of practices whereas participatory research is concerned with equity, self-reliance, and oppression problems.

Participatory research takes place within a force field of power relations in which conflicts of interest often create resistance to the research. Participatory researchers assume that they will be resisted from above (i.e., powerful vested interests), whereas traditional action researchers are often consultants who are hired by the powerful.

While less overtly political than Freire, Heron's (1996) experiential approach to action research—which he terms *co-operative inquiry*—emphasizes the intersubjectivity among researchers and participants.

> In meeting people, there is the possibility of reciprocal participative knowing, and unless this is truly mutual, we don't properly know the other. The reality of the other is found in the fullness of our open relation (Buber, 1937), when we each engage in our mutual participation. Hence the importance of co-operative inquiry with other persons involving dialogue, parity and reciprocity in all its phases. (p. 11)

Although Freire was influenced by Marx and liberation theology, and Heron by humanistic psychology, both are concerned with using participatory research as a way to highlight paths toward greater humanization and away from dehumanization. In both models, our ontological vocation is to become more fully human.

Participatory Evaluation

In chapter 6, we describe a PAR project that began as a contract to do program evaluation. The field of evaluation has long supported approaches that blend in many ways with PAR. During the 1960s and 1970s, the field of program evaluation was widely criticized for being methodologically narrow, irrelevant to those being evaluated, unfair in favoring influential people and bureaucratic sponsors, and narrow in the types of questions that were asked (Weiss, 1987). Stake (1975) used the term *responsive evaluation* to describe a shift toward a more reflective, participatory approach to evaluation.

> An educational evaluation is *responsive evaluation* if it orients more directly to program activities than to program intents; responds to audience requirements of information; and if the different value-perspectives present are referred to in reporting the success and failure of the program. (p. 14)

The increasing acceptance of including stakeholders in evaluations led to its use by the federal government to evaluate programs like Jesse Jackson's PUSH/Excel (Farrar & House, 1986). While the results were mixed, evaluators continued to refine more participatory and utilization-focused approaches (Patton, 1996). What Guba and Lincoln (1989) call fourth-generation evaluation is barely distinguishable from the tenets of PAR. For a participatory evaluation dissertation, see Seigart (1999).

In international development work, a form of participatory evaluation known as Participatory Rural Appraisal (PRA) has gained widespread support. Although there are different views of PRA, the primary source for understanding its theory and practice is the work of Robert Chambers (1994, 1997). PRA practitioners struggle with many of the dilemmas of participatory evaluation research, discussed above, that is sponsored by powerful external agencies. For examples of dissertations that address PRA, see Pelletier (2001), Perez (2000), Toness (2002), and Tuttle (2003).

Action Research in Education

In the field of education, action research has enjoyed widespread success, both as an individual route to professional development and as a collaborative route to professional and institutional change. Because so many educators are themselves in graduate programs, many have done theses and dissertations as action researchers working on the inside of their organizations. As we will discuss in the next chapter, this insider status creates a set of dilemmas that are quite different from PAR, in which the outside change agent collaborates with insiders.

While action research in education has evolved differently than in other fields, its popularity has created a rich debate that can inform dilemmas encountered by action researchers in all fields. In fact, action research has become so popular in education, particularly as a mode of professional development and "data-based decision making," that, as with the democratic workplace movement, there is much concern that it may become a form of domestication rather than empowerment.

The theoretical foundations of action research in education are grounded in the importance that John Dewey gave to human experience in the generation of knowledge. From Dewey, it was a short step to the notion of taking the professional experience of teachers and other practitioners and using it as a source of knowledge about teaching. Schon's (1983) notion of the reflective practitioner and professional learning owe a similar debt to Dewey. Unfortunately, during the second half of the twentieth century, this simple logic has been largely drowned out by the fixation in education on using positivist research methods that enjoyed greater legitimacy in the natural and social sciences, as well as psychology—education's parent discipline.

The idea of educational practitioners doing research in schools goes back at least as far as the late nineteenth and early twentieth century with the movement for the scientific study of education. Teachers were viewed as the front line of data gatherers for a massive research movement that saw teachers as researchers, working scientifically in their classroom laboratories (McKernan, 1988). Although this vision of teachers as researchers never materialized, it is interesting to note that within this model, teachers were allocated the role of carrying out research in their classrooms that was designed by university researchers. This vision of teachers as researchers tended to view teachers as mere gatherers of data that could be analyzed statistically.

As early as 1926, Buckingham (cited in McKernan, 1988) recognized the potential of qualitative, case study research: "Among the many types of research work available to teachers, the making of case studies is by no means unimportant" (p. 176). The hierarchical relations between universities and schools reflected in most of this early work on practitioner research continues to be a source of tension today.

Overlapping with this scientific movement in education was the progressive movement inspired by John Dewey. Referring to Dewey's contribution to action research, McKernan (1988) states:

> In *Logic: The Theory of Inquiry,* he once again argues that there must be a unity of the structure of inquiry in both common sense and science. He promoted logic as a method of scientific thinking and problem resolution. Later Action Researchers, such as Lewin, Corey, and Taba, also followed these steps of reflective thinking, thus demonstrating the linkage of the scientific method with Action Research. (p. 176)

For a more complete discussion of action research and the Progressive Era, see Schubert and Lopez-Schubert (1997).

During the early 1950s, action research was promoted in the field of education principally by Corey (1949, 1953, 1954) at Columbia Teachers College, who believed that teachers would likely find the results of their own research more useful than that of "outsiders" and, thus, would be more likely to question current curricular practices. Corey was the executive officer of the Horace Mann-Lincoln Institute of School Experimentation, which had been founded at Teachers College by H.L. Caswell. Under Corey's direction, members of the Institute's staff collaborated on research with classroom teachers. In his 1953 book, Corey published several of these studies and a summary of what he called the "cooperative Action Research movement." Arthur Foshay (1993) a participant in the movement (Foshay & Wann, 1953), describes the rather sudden demise of action research in education.

> The chief limitation of cooperative Action Research, from the point of view of the educational researchers of the time, was that it was not possible to generalize from the examined population to others, because no attempt was made to see whether the examined population was representative of a larger population. In addition, since much of the research was designed and carried out by classroom teachers, who were not trained in research, the data often were flawed. For these reasons the movement was ridiculed in the publications of the American Educational Research Association (AERA), and it did not spread. It disappeared as the members of the Institute staff scattered with the passage of time. (Foshay, 1993, p. 3)

It is not surprising, given the general hostility that educational researchers in the 1950s felt toward nonpositivist research of any kind, that action research would be ridiculed and judged by positivist standards. By the end of the 1950s, action research had not only declined in the field of education but in the social sciences as well. Sanford (1970), in an article titled "Whatever Happened to Action Research?" suggested that funding agencies wanted more basic research and that an increasing split between science and practice led to the cult of the expert (Lindblom & Cohen, 1979) and the top-down, social engineering mentality of the period.

Although action research never totally disappeared, interest waned during the 1960s—a decade in which adherence to the cult of social engineering reached its height. The late British researcher Lawrence Stenhouse is usually credited with renewing interest in action research in Britain during the 1970s.

The Teacher-as-Researcher Movement in Britain

Although there had been much discussion throughout the twentieth century of the idea of school practitioners doing research within their own sites, there had generally been more talk than action. A teacher research movement that began in Britain during the late 1960s began to change this. This movement is most often associated with the work of Lawrence Stenhouse, who established the Center for Applied Research in Education (CARE) at East Anglia University and, later, with the work of John Elliott and Clem Adelman with the Ford Teaching Project.

Elliott (1991) makes the case that, in reality, teacher research began as a teacher-led curriculum reform movement that grew out of concern by teachers over the forced implementation of behavioral objectives in curriculum and Britain's tracked educational system. Elliott (1991) describes his own partici-pation in the teacher-as-researcher movement in England during the 1960s:

> Curriculum practices were not derived (by us) from curriculum theories gener-ated and tested independently of that practice. They constituted means by which we generated and tested our own and each other's theories. Practices took on the status of hypotheses to be tested. So we collected empirical data about their effects, and used it as evidence in which to ground our theorizing with each other in the context of collegial accountability. We didn't call it research, let alone Action Research. This articulation came much later as the world of academia responded to change in schools. But the concept of teaching as reflexive practice and a form of educational inquiry was tacitly and intuitively grasped in our experience of the innovation process. Our research was by no means systematic. It occurred as a response to particular questions and issues as they arose. (p. 8)

The heyday of action research in Britain saw a teacher research movement develop in the schools as well as in a series of large, state-funded collaborative action research projects. During the 1970s and 1980s, a lively debate took place in Britain over a number of issues in action research. Among them were a search for a guiding paradigm (Altricher & Posch, 1989), the political problems of promoting action research within institutions that do not want to look at themselves too closely (Holly, 1989), and the usefulness of more quantitative approaches to action research (Harwood, 1991). One of the most interesting critiques was that of feminist action researchers.

Feminist researchers involved in the Girls and Occupational Choice Project (Chisholm, 1990; Weiner, 1989) and Girls in Science and Technology (Whyte, 1987) argued that action research was being turned into a project in social engineering and was losing its "emancipatory" potential. German femi-nist action researcher Maria Mies (cited in Chisholm, 1990) argued that the radical potential of action research was lost when it was turned into a recipe and controlled by state agencies:

> [Early on] "action" was interpreted not as socially liberating and dynamic praxis, but rather, in a manner observable in many activist groupings where precise short-term goals are set, as a narrow pragmatism. The same would appear to be

true for what is termed "Action Research," which typically comprises planned intervention in specific social contexts, mostly under the control and direction of state agencies and monitored by researchers—in other words, a sort of social engineering. (p. 255)

This concern with moving action research beyond narrow pragmatism and planned interventions by external agencies was taken up earlier by a group of Australians led by Stephen Kemmis, who spent time with British action researchers at East Anglia (Tripp, 1990). Carr and Kemmis's (1986) book *Becoming Critical* challenged older models of action research as essentially conservative and positivistic. In a later article, Carr (1989) reasserts, "In theory, Action Research is only intelligible as an attempt to revive those forms of democratic dialogue and reflective theorizing which under the impact of positivism have been rendered marginal" (p. 89). He is concerned that as action research becomes more methodologically sophisticated and technically proficient, it will lose its critical edge.

Two booklets that had a powerful effect on action researchers in education were Kemmis and McTaggart's (1987) *The Action Research Planner,* a user-friendly introduction to the action research spiral, and Kemmis's (1982) *The Action Research Reader,* a compilation of critical action research studies.

The Practitioner Research Movement in North America

Although the teacher researcher movement in North America occurred later than in Britain and Latin America, it was not derivative of either movement, nor was it a reappropriation of the North American action research movement of the 1940s and 1950s. The Center for Applied Research in Education at East Anglia in Britain and the work of Paulo Freire inspired many North American academics and some teachers, but the movement among North American teachers to do research began with a unique set of circumstances.

1. The dominance of the quantitative, positivistic paradigm of research in education was challenged by qualitative, case study, and ethnographic research from the late 1960s on. Because they more closely resemble the narrative forms already used by practitioners to communicate their craft knowledge, making qualitative forms of research legitimate helped open the door for practitioners to experiment with more systematic qualitative approaches in studying their practice.

2. Research on successful school change efforts and schools as contexts for teachers' professional work began to report that school-based problem-solving approaches to change were more likely to be successfully implemented than large, federally funded, outside-in initiatives (Lieberman & Miller, 1984). These findings spawned

a large number of collaborative, or interactive, research and development efforts in which educational practitioners were invited to work alongside research and development experts in implementing programs and improving practices. (For accounts of these collaborative research projects, see Griffin, Lieberman, & Jacullo-Noto, 1982; Oja & Ham, 1984; Tikunoff, Ward, & Griffin, 1979.)

3. The increased deskilling of teachers and the dissemination of teacher-proof curricula spawned an effort on the part of educational practitioners to repro-fessionalize teaching and to reclaim teachers' knowledge about practice as valid. Donald Schon's (1983) book *The Reflective Practitioner* encouraged practition-ers to begin to tap into their store of professional knowledge in order to make it explicit and share it with other practitioners. From the notion of reflective practice, it was only a short step to that of action research, which became linked to an overall attempt by educational practitioners to reassert their profession-alism. The Boston Women's Teachers' Group's report *The Effect of Teaching on Teachers* (Freedman, Jackson, & Boles, 1986) describes the structural condi-tions and isolation of teachers' work that makes professionalism difficult. They point out that teachers work "in an institution which supposedly prepares its clients for adulthood, but which views those entrusted with this task as inca-pable of mature judgment" (Freedman, Jackson, & Boles, 1986, p. 263). Liston and Zeichner (1991), in reviewing the group's work, point out that their research was used to

> combat the individualistic bias in the school reform movement of the 1980s, which served to direct teachers' sense of frustration with and anger about their work away from a critical analysis of schools as institutions to a preoccupation with their own individual failures. (p. 150)

These problems have increased in the wake of the omnibus No Child Left Behind educational reform legislation, signed by President Bush on January 8, 2002, which gives these deskilling tendencies the force of law (McNeil, 2000). Its social engineering tendencies, obsession with testing, and narrow forms of accountability have decreased professional autonomy for teachers and admin-istrators. Under the influence of such regimes, forms of action research are captured by the technical knowledge interests described later in this chapter.

4. Encouraged by the pioneering work of Atwell (1982), Brookline Teacher Research Seminar (2003), Goswami and Stillman (1987), Graves (1981a, 1981b), Myers (1985), and the Bay Area Writing Project, language arts teachers led the way in doing teacher research and writing about it from an insider per-spective. Not only have they used student writing as data, but also they have written case studies of a variety of issues in the teaching of writing. Because of these teachers' own commitment to writing, they have tended to lead the way in writing and publishing accounts of their experiences as teacher researchers. (See Ballenger, 1992, 1998; Bissex & Bullock, 1987; Brookline Teacher Research Seminar, 2003; Gallas, 1993, 1997, 2003; Goswami & Schultz, 1993; Martin, 2001, for examples.) The increasing importance of Vygotskian, sociocultural approaches to literacy have also encouraged greater collaboration among researchers and practitioners (Lee, Smagorinsky, Pea, Brown, & Heath, 1999).

5. Many university teacher education programs and university/school collaborations began to emphasize teacher research. One of the best known efforts to incorporate teacher research into a teacher education program is that of Ken Zeichner and others at the University of Wisconsin (Liston & Zeichner, 1991). Susan Noffke, Jennifer Gore, and Marie Brennan, all former university supervisors in the elementary teacher education program at Wisconsin, have documented the uses of practitioner research in the training of teachers (Noffke & Brennan, 1991; Zeichner, 1981–1982).

Programs of this kind are becoming more common in colleges of education and promise to have an important impact on moving teacher and administrative preparation programs toward a more reflective model. For accounts of other similar programs and discussions of the role of action research in teacher education and school-university collaborations, see Christman et al. (1995); Clift, Veal, Holland, Johnson, and McCarthy (1995); Gitlin et al. (1992); Johnson (2002); Moller (1998); Sirotnik (1988); Smith-Maddox (1999); and Whitford, Schlechty, and Shelor (1989).

6. The school restructuring movement of the 1980s began to propose restructuring schools to create conditions that nurture teacher inquiry and reflection. The Holmes Group's (1990) *Tomorrow's Schools* contains a chapter dedicated to schools as "centers for reflection and inquiry." This chapter covers themes first reported in Schaefer's 1967 book, *The School as a Center of Inquiry*. The notion of schools as communities of learners has grown over the past two decades (Rogoff, Turkanis, & Bartlett, 2001). Many independent collaborative efforts to restructure schools have included practitioner research as an aspect of teacher empowerment. In Georgia, the League of Professional Schools has made action research a key component in the move to shared governance and school renewal (Glickman, 1993). The Coalition of Essential Schools is founded on the notion of ongoing inquiry and reflection, and attempts to build these habits of mind in students. These types of reform movements have promise to make practitioner research more legitimate.

The Danger of Co-optation

Even before the deskilling tendencies of the No Child Left Behind legislation, there has been great concern about using action research as a motivational tool that focuses on the best means to ends determined elsewhere.

When the critical dimension of teacher research is negated, the teacher-as-researcher movement can become quite a trivial enterprise. Uncritical educational Action Research seeks direct applications of information gleaned to specific situations—a cookbook style of technical thinking is encouraged. . . . Such thinking does not allow for complex reconceptualizations of knowledge and as a result fails to understand the ambiguities and the ideological structures of the classroom. [In this way] teacher research is co-opted, its democratic edge is blunted. It becomes a popular grassroots movement that can be supported by the power hierarchy—it does not threaten, nor is it threatened. Asking trivial questions, the movement presents no radical challenge or offers no transformative vision of educational purpose, as it acts in ignorance of deep structures of schooling. (Kincheloe, 1991, p. 83)

In a similar vein, Miller (1990) recounts how she and a group of teachers in a research study group struggled with this very issue of expanding the focus of practitioner research so as to become "challengers" of nonresponsive educational institutions. One teacher researcher in the group asked the following question:

Do you think that we could just turn into another form, an acceptable professional form of empowerment? Well, what I mean is that nothing would please some administrators I know more than to think that we were doing "research" in their terms. That's what scares me about the phrase "teacher-as-researcher" these days—too packaged. People buy back into the very system that shuts them down. That immediately eliminates the critical perspectives that we're working on, I'm afraid. But I'm still convinced that if enough people do this, we could get to a point of seeing at least a bigger clearing for us. (p. 114)

As Schon (1983) has pointed out, social institutions are characterized by *dynamic conservatism*. It is dynamic in that it constantly pulls practitioners back to a status quo that, as noted by Argyris et al. (1985) above, consists of norms, rules, skills, and values that become so omnipresent as to be taken for granted and to go unchallenged. Action research can either reproduce those norms, rules, skills, and values or it can challenge them. However, practitioners intuitively know that when they challenge the norms, the institutions' dynamic conservatism will respond in a defensive, self-protective manner.

Practitioners will have to make their peace with how much of a challenger of the status quo they wish to be. Some are more skillful and in stronger positions to take stands on issues than others. However, if action research is not done with a critical spirit, it runs the risk of simply legitimating what may be—from the perspective of equity considerations—unacceptable social arrangements.

Action Research as Self-Study and Autoethnography

Some writers on action research criticize its tendency to privilege the group over the individual (Webb, 1996). Whitehead (1991, cited in Webb, 1996), for example, promotes action research as a self-reflective process focused on the individual.

I believe that the incorporation of 'I' as a living contradiction in explanations for the educational development of individuals, has distinguished an original contribution to the Action Research movement. . . . I experience problems or concerns when some of my values are denied in my practice; I imagine ways of improving my practice and choose a course of action; I act and gather evidence which will enable me to make a judgment on the effectiveness of my actions; I evaluate the outcomes of my actions; I modify my concerns, ideas and action in the light of my evaluation. (p. 94; see also McNiff & Whitehead, 2000)

This focus on the individual practitioner follows the lead of Schon (1983) in attempting to understand how practitioners learn their craft. A focus on one's own personal and professional selves is a form of action research usually called *self-study* (Bullough & Pinnegar, 2001) or *autoethnography* (Bochner & Ellis, 2002; Reed-Danahay, 1997).

Emerging Approaches to Action Research

Action research has gained its greatest acceptance in applied fields such as organizational development, education, social work, criminology, nursing, public health, international development, and agriculture. Among social science disciplines, psychology has tended to marginalize most nonpositivist approaches to research, even qualitative, interpretive approaches largely accepted in other disciplines. Nevertheless, action research has gained a small foothold among some psychologists who see the relationality that action research builds among researchers and participants as an advantage rather than a threat to validity (Tolman & Brydon-Miller, 2001). Tandon, Kelly, and Mock (2001) refer to this as "ecological validity."

By including the Developing Communities Project (DCP) representatives throughout this work, the research team made a continuous effort to construct a genuine, trusting partnership between DCP and the University of Illinois, Chicago research team that would enhance this work's ecological validity (Bronfenbrenner, 1979; Chavis, Stucky, & Wandersman, 1983; Kelly, 1999), or the degree to which the constructs and products of this work are relevant to DCP. (p. 201)

This growing legitimacy for action research in the field of psychology promises to contribute to processes of personal and social transformation.

Feminist and feminist, antiracist approaches to action research have produced many dissertations that have pushed the boundaries of PAR, critiquing dominant paradigm thinking that creeps into even more critical approaches. As discussed above, feminists and critical theorists both have critiqued the social engineering tendencies of turning action research into a codified and packaged professional and organizational development strategy. Maguire (1987b) and others have pointed out the lack of female voices in the international debate about action research. Racial discourses have yet to be examined in depth in action research (Bell, 2001), but with the advent of critical race theory, such critiques are likely to become more common (see Chavez, Duran, Baker, Avila, & Wallerstein, 2003). Since PAR is linked to international development projects, insights from postcolonial theory might also be useful. Some of the dissertations listed under PRA provide the beginnings of a postcolonial critique. For examples of feminist and feminist, antiracist action research dissertations, see Asten (1993), Brown (1993), Goldin Rosenberg (1999), Maguire (1987a), Martin (1998).

The Knowledge Interests of Action Research

There is a built-in conservatism in much action research, particularly research done in institutions by practitioners, who are immersed in a reified and naturalized world in which common sense is constructed. Furthermore, role expectations for legitimation of the status quo are embedded in most institutions. This problem, which has been noted by many advocates of organizational learning and critical reflection (Argyris et al., 1985; Argyris & Schon, 1974; Robinson, 1993; Tripp, 1990, 1994) requires some mechanism that can problematize those taken-for-granted aspects of organizational life. These issues are linked to a long tradition of analyses of sources of distortion in social inquiry beginning with the shadows in Plato's cave, Freud's subconscious, Marx's false consciousness, and Gramsci's hegemony, through more recent versions such as Habermas's distorted communication, Lindblom's impairments to inquiry, and Argyris's theories-in-use. Many writers on action research have taken a critical approach to action research, arguing that there is nothing in current approaches to action research or reflective practice that might interrupt the mere reproduction of current "best" practices that support the current social order (Anderson & Herr, 1999; Carr & Kemmis, 1986; Tripp, 1990; Zeichner & Noffke, 2002). Although there is much talk about reflection and reflexivity, few accounts of how this is done in action research exist (see Hall, 1996).

The author most cited in this regard is Jurgens Habermas (1971), who argued that knowledge production is never neutral, but rather is always pursued with some interest in mind. Habermas also has argued that communication within any public sphere is always distorted through the relations of power that form the context of the communicative act.

While all research traditions have some set of criteria for determining the validity of truth claims, most research traditions advocate a disinterested stance toward the generation of knowledge. Critical and feminist approaches to research tend to take a more normative position (Anderson, 1989), as do Argyris et al. (1985), who suggest "that action science is an exemplar of critical theory as formulated by the Frankfurt School. A critical theory seeks to engage human agents in public self-reflection in order to transform their world" (p. 2). Kemmis (2002) provides a much more in-depth discussion of applications of Habermas to action research, and Fraser (1996) provides a feminist critique of his theory of communicative action.

Habermas (1971) pointed out that knowledge and human interests were inseparable. He argued against the claim of the objectivist that valid knowledge could only be generated through methodologies that were empirical-analytical in nature. These research methods attempted to separate what was considered the bias of the researcher from the subject being investigated. However, Habermas insisted that such a separation was an illusion that is ultimately shattered through the process of self-reflection. He maintained that because knowledge was generated through the interest of the mind, knowledge and interest are forever linked and cannot be unattached. In refuting the claim of objectivism as the sole pathway to valid knowledge, he presents three distinct "interests" of the researcher in the pursuit of knowledge generation: technical, practical, and emancipatory. Each interest establishes an orientation and an associated research methodology.

Technical interest focuses upon human desire to take control over the natural and social realm. Knowledge generated through this orientation historically assumes a disinterested stance toward the topic being investigated, and knowledge generated takes on the form of causal explanations and instrumentation. *Practical* interest refers to an orientation toward gaining understanding through interpretation. The researcher engaged in the pursuit of practical interest employs interpretive methodologies—primarily hermeneutic interpretation—in an effort to provide understanding of a given situation. Consequently, interpretative understanding seeks to generate knowledge that informs and guides practical judgments. Methods associated with the practical interest include hermeneutical methods such as textual, conversation, and discourse analysis, as well as ethnographic and other qualitative methods.

An *emancipatory* interest orients the researcher toward the release of human potential and the investigation of ideology and power within the organization and society. The ultimate goal of this kind of research is that of the "emancipation of participants from the dictates or compulsions of tradition, precedent, habit, coercion or self-deception" (Carr & Kemmis, 1986). These are thought to be subtle and deeply embedded into the belief structure of the organization and, through the process of critical self-reflection, they can be accessed and surfaced for examination ultimately leading to transformation.

While Habermas's knowledge interests have been criticized, particularly Carr and Kemmis's appropriation of his work to action research (see Gibson, 1985; Webb, 1996; Whitehead & Lomax, 1987), we find his distinctions useful in guarding against the potential for action research to unreflectively reproduce current practices. The notion of emancipatory knowledge interests leads to the

Table 2.1   Continuum of Intentionality Based on Habermas's Knowledge
                   Interests

Knowledge Interest	Research Aims
Technical (uses empirical analytic science and instrumental reason)	*Explanation* through empirical facts and generalizations
Practical/Communicative (uses hermeneutical/interpretive sciences)	Illumination of *understandings* of participants
Emancipatory (uses critical reflective/ action sciences)	*Critical reflection*—how understandings are constrained or distorted by power relations

potential for critical reflection and the problematization of current practices as well as one's own unexamined assumptions (Tripp, 1994). In other words, it stresses problem posing rather than merely problem solving. See Table 2.1 for a summary of Habermas's knowledge interests.

Our point here is not to disqualify any particular methodology for action research. For example, while certain methodologies tend to be associated with certain knowledge interests, we don't see a conflict in using statistical methods toward emancipatory ends, as long as it forms part of a cycle of ongoing critical reflection.

Our emphasis in this chapter has been on presenting alternative criteria for goodness for the unique purposes and positionalities of action research. We hope we have provided dissertation writers with some conceptual tools for thinking through both the limitations and strengths of their methodology.

3

The Continuum of Positionality in Action Research

This chapter will discuss a continuum of positions researchers take, from being an insider to being an outsider to the setting under study. Much action research is centrally concerned with these issues of the relationship between outsiders and insiders, since clarity about them is necessary for thinking through issues of research validity as well as research ethics. Traditionally, action researchers were seen as outside change agents. It was assumed that the research was initiated by an outsider, and the central issue was how to involve insiders in the research to a greater extent than with traditional research. Much of this research was—and continues to be—contract or evaluation research, and it was usually funded to solve a particular problem or evaluate a particular program. Master's theses and doctoral dissertations from this action research approach are often done in applied fields that prepare graduates to work collaboratively in areas such as international development, community psychology, social work, health promotion, and other fields.

With the advent of highly educated professionals who have acquired research skills and are enrolled in doctorate programs, action research dissertations are often done by organizational insiders who see it as a way to deepen their own reflection on practice toward problem solving and professional development. In such cases, the researcher and the practitioner may be one and the same. Research by Anderson and Jones (2000) on dissertations in educational leadership suggests that these practitioners were partly motivated by the convenience of studying their own site, where they had a deep level of tacit knowledge. However, more important, they wanted their research to make a contribution to their own setting and clients. In many cases, they wanted to use it to empower themselves professionally and personally and to bring about organizational change.

Marilyn Cochran-Smith and Susan Lytle's (1993) important book *Inside/ Outside: Teacher Research and Knowledge* was one of the first to lay out in detail the possibilities and dilemmas of this type of insider research. The issue for many teachers was that knowledge about teaching was being generated exclusively by academic researchers, and that this knowledge was not viewed as useful to the teachers themselves. Clandinin and Connelly (1995) argued that outsider knowledge was often experienced by practitioners as a "rhetoric of conclusions," which entered the practitioners' professional landscape through informational conduits that funneled propositional and theoretical knowledge to them with little understanding that their landscape was personal, contextual, subjective, temporal, historical, and relational among people. While insiders can do research without outsiders, insiders doing dissertations have a formal committee of outsiders they can rely on for methodological guidance. Besides a dissertation committee, most action researchers also seek independent *critical friends* who can help them problematize the taken-for-granted aspects of their setting. While insider and outsider positions are at the extremes of the continuum, many studies are done by true collaborations among insiders and outsiders. These studies are known as participatory or collaborative research; Bartunek and Louis (1996) use the term *insider/outsider team research.*

We dedicate an entire chapter to the issue of positionality because the degree to which researchers position themselves as insiders or outsiders will determine how they frame epistemological, methodological, and ethical issues in the dissertation. As faculty who advise action research dissertations, we have looked in vain for sources that help students think through how their decisions about positionality influence the many other decisions they will make throughout the study.

Besides the issue of being insiders or outsiders to the setting under study, there are other ways to think about positionality. Collins (1990) uses the term *outsider within* to refer to the particular perspective on society that being black and female gives her. In chapter 6, we discuss Lynne Mock's relationship to her African American participants. As an African American, she is racially an insider, but as a university researcher, she is an outsider. At the end of this chapter, we will take up in more detail these other ways researchers and participants position themselves.

The continuum and implications of positionality presented in Table 3.1. are, in part, the product of a study of numerous action research studies in education that included dissertations, published articles, and conference papers (Anderson & Jones, 2000). The original goal of the study was to explore the potential of action research studies as a new source of professional knowledge in the field of education (more specifically, educational leadership). For this book, we have expanded our database beyond educational leadership and explored implications of each position for the validity of action research studies, as well as the unique ethical dilemmas that arise for each position.

Table 3.1   Continuum and Implications of Positionality

Insider (1) _____ *(2)* _____ *(3)* _____ *(4)* _____ *(5)* _____ *(6) Outsider*

Positionality of Researcher	Validity Criteria	Contributes to:	Traditions
1. Insider[a] (researcher studies own self/ practice)	Anderson & Herr (1999), Bullough & Pinnegar (2001), Connelly & Clandinin (1990)	Knowledge base, Improved/critiqued practice, Self/ professional transformation	Practitioner research, Autobiography, Narrative research, Self-study
2. Insider in collaboration with other insiders	Heron (1996), Saavedra (1996)	Knowledge base, Improved/critiqued practice, Professional/ organizational transformation	Feminist consciousness raising groups, Inquiry/Study groups, Teams
3. Insider(s) in collaboration with outsider(s)	Anderson & Herr (1999), Heron (1996), Saavedra (1996)	Knowledge base, Improved/critiqued practice, Professional/ organizational transformation	Inquiry/Study groups
4. Reciprocal collaboration (insider-outsider teams)	Anderson & Herr (1999), Bartunek & Louis (1996)	Knowledge base, Improved/critiqued practice, Professional/ organizational transformation	Collaborative forms of participatory action research that achieve equitable power relations
5. Outsider(s) in collabo-ration with insider(s)	Anderson & Herr (1999), Bradbury & Reason (2001a), Heron (1996)	Knowledge base, Improved/critiqued practice, Organizational development/ transformation	Mainstream change agency: consultancies, industrial democracy, organizational learning; Radical change: community empowerment (Paulo Freire)
6. Outsider(s) studies insider(s)	Campbell & Stanley (1963), Lincoln & Guba (1985)	Knowledge base	University-based, academic research on action research methods or action research projects

a. A flawed and deceptive version of this is when an insider studies his or her own site but fails to position himself or herself as an insider to the setting (*outsider within*).

While the researcher's positionality in relation to the setting is important, it is often no simple matter to define one's position. Some researchers who are outsiders to the setting have little knowledge of it, while others may have extensive—and often firsthand—knowledge of the setting. For instance, some researchers studying social service agencies may have previously been social workers. Many educational action researchers studying schools may have been teachers. An outside researcher studying a particular Puerto Rican community may be Puerto Rican and may have once lived in the community.

Furthermore, participatory action researchers, who tend to be outsiders to the setting under study, report that their relationship to participants can shift throughout a study and can vary for different parts of the study. For instance, participation may be stronger at the problem-posing and data-gathering part of the study than at the write-up and dissemination part. To further complicate matters, insiders to a setting do not have direct access to the "truth" of the setting. Theirs is merely one truth among many.

In the following sections, we have attempted to make some sense of a continuum of positionalities using somewhat oversimplified categories. As we have pointed out, one's positionality doesn't fall out in neat categories and might even shift during the study. Researchers will have to figure out the nuances of how they position themselves with regard to their setting and participants. The reader will find more examples from the field of education on the insider end of the continuum, because insider practitioner research is most common in education, although it is becoming increasingly common in fields such as nursing and social work. On the outsider end of the continuum, we provide more examples from organizational and international development, public health, and applied sociology and psychology, particularly community psychology.

Insider: Researcher Studies Own Self/Practice

If we begin on the far left of the continuum, category 1 in Table 3.1, we have dissertations in which insiders, either alone or in collaboration with other insiders, are researching their own practice and/or practice setting. It is useful to discuss the lone insider researcher separate from an insider group of researchers as we have done in Table 3.1. While one's practice cannot be separated from the setting within which it takes place, a focus on one's own practice versus the actions initiated within the setting is an important conceptual distinction. A focus on one's own personal and professional self is a form of action research usually called self-study (Bullough & Pinnegar, 2001) or autoethnography (Bochner & Ellis, 2002; Reed-Danahay, 1997). Jack Whitehead's website (www.bath.ac.uk/~edsajw) at the University of Bath in England provides an excellent overview and examples of theses and dissertations done from this vantage point. Such studies add to the literature on reflective practice and professional learning (Schon, 1983, 1987). In these cases, there is a greater emphasis on narrative, self-reflective methods.

On the other hand, practitioner researchers often want to study the outcomes of a program or actions in their own setting, much like an internal evaluation study. These studies often rely on more traditional qualitative and quantitative methods of data gathering. As we will discuss in this chapter, a common mistake in this type of research is to treat one's personal and professional self as an outside observer rather than as an insider committed to the success of the actions under study. We find it is difficult and perhaps deceptive to attempt to separate the study of one's self and practice from the study of the outcomes of actions initiated in a setting. If a researcher is studying a program that is his or her "baby," then the tendency for self-promotion may be too great to overcome. In such cases, an outsider should be brought in to do the study, even if it means finding another dissertation topic.

The following excerpt from Moyra Evans's (1995) dissertation illustrates the impulse to self-reflection that often leads to an action research study. At the time of the study, Evans was a deputy head (what would be called an assistant or vice principal in the U.S.) of a school in Britain.

"What are you doing?" I asked George, one of the other deputy heads, one Wednesday afternoon at about five o'clock. "Oh, this and that," he replied. He stopped doing this or that, and tried to put his mind to talking to me.

"I don't seem to have anything to do," I said, naively. I had only been there a few days. He looked at me as if he were about to launch into a diatribe about what he had to do, and then thought better of it.

"You will soon" was all he said, soothingly, and turned back to his pieces of paper.

Gradually, I became the proud receiver of pieces of paper. At first they only trickled in. I felt very important, and looked for places to file them. That seemed to be a useful task—to update the previous Deputy's filing cabinet. I thought I would just leave last year's papers there and then add my own. But it wasn't that easy. I couldn't work out why papers relating to twenty years ago were still there. I made an early decision to throw them all out and start again.

I developed a good system, I had a space for everything, and for the first three weeks or so, every letter or document was put away. The papers covered a much wider range of items than those I had received when I was a Senior Teacher elsewhere. I realized that the Head and three Deputies had copies of practically every document that was generated in the school, and that this was a good way of ensuring communications were effective. I certainly couldn't complain that I had been left out; neither could I complain that I didn't know something, because the chances were, that if I had read my paperwork, I would know.

Lessons, marking, administration, meetings, planning—all gathered pace, and eventually I was caught up in the race with everyone else. It was tremendously exciting and I felt very privileged to be at the heart of the management of the institution. I enjoyed talking about how we should go about achieving our aims and planning all of this with various groups of people in the school. I enjoyed doing the work—"getting my hands dirty" is the expression we used.

I remember my life as being on a series of interconnecting treadmills. The momentum had increased so much that I felt I was running along from one rung to the next, jumping from one wheel to another—just keeping going, not pausing to see the scenery. I had always liked running, and reckoned to be good, but eventually, I became a little disenchanted. I wanted to get off. I wanted to stop and see what was happening around me. (p. 97)

We cite the above passage from Evans's (1995) dissertation because it captures the spirit of practitioners' need to make meaning of their practice. Schon (1983) used the notion of the *reflective practitioner* to describe those practitioners who "learn to learn" about their practice and therefore become better practitioners. In a sense, these types of dissertations are insider case studies of practitioner learning that both become a form of professional development for the researcher and provide case study data on how practitioners learn and grow in different professional contexts.

Some academics don't take dissertations very seriously as sources of knowledge because they are seen as being done by amateur researchers who are just learning their craft. However, this type of action research dissertation is more than an amateur researcher demonstrating a certain level of competence in doing research. It is an account of how one practitioner went about learning his or her craft and what was learned in the process. Such insider accounts generate important knowledge to be shared among practitioners, just as case studies reported by academic researchers do. In fact, they begin to build a knowledge base that can inform the research community about the actions and beliefs of practitioners—a knowledge base that is otherwise unavailable.

This type of self-reflective action research is always written up in the first person. Evans's (1995) narrative has characteristics of a story, with elements of humor and irony and a narrative hook that leads the reader into wanting to read more. Practitioners tend to use narrative and story as a way to communicate professional knowledge, which makes it particularly appropriate for action research. Unlike action research studies that use ethnographic and behavioral science methods, self-studies often use journals and diaries as major sources of data. Insider researchers have unique dilemmas. A simple logistical dilemma is that they can't be in two places at once. Practitioners don't have the luxury of the ethnographer, who can take copious field notes, write them up, and transcribe interviews. Using the ethnographic approach places practitioners in a logistically untenable position because they can't work and record data at the same time (Anderson, Herr, & Nihlen, 1994). A few accounts, primarily in education, exist of how practitioners have adapted traditional methods to their own contexts (Anderson, Herr, & Nihlen, 1994; Cochran-Smith & Lytle, 1993; Hubbard & Power, 1999). As practitioner research continues to become more prevalent in fields such as nursing and social work, we anticipate that similar accounts will be produced for those unique contexts.

The tacit knowledge that a practitioner acquires over months and years of working in a site raises both logistical and epistemological issues. Logistically, this tacit knowledge is an advantage in that it would have to be reproduced from scratch through ethnographic observation at a new site. However, it raises epistemological problems in the sense that unexamined, tacit knowledge of a site tends to be impressionistic, full of bias, prejudice, and unexamined impressions and assumptions that need to be surfaced and examined. Furthermore, insiders, because they are often true believers in their particular practices, are too often tempted to put a positive spin on their data. For this reason, mechanisms for dealing with bias need to be employed. (See chapter 4 for validity criteria.)

We will discuss the issue of bias in more detail, but one way to deal with bias is to acknowledge one's presence in the study and build in self-reflection. In the following dissertation abstract, Fecho (1995) describes how he went about doing a study in his own classroom in which he wanted to do ethnographic research while acknowledging his own presence as teacher and researcher. He frames his research as a "hybrid between the traditional dissertation study and studies carried out by teachers on their own practice" (p. 2).

This study was a year-long investigation into the work and attitudes associated with language and language study of the teacher and students in a North Philadelphia classroom. The text describes the complex evolution of a class where language was made problematic and students were encouraged to raise and investigate questions about the roles language played in their lives. It was conducted as a form of teacher research using qualitative methods and, as such, represents a hybrid between the traditional dissertation study and studies carried out by teachers on their own practice. It argues that the study benefits from both paradigms in that it is responsive to the scope, knowledge base, and rigor of academic research while documenting the practice of the teacher from an emic, or insider, perspective—a perspective too rare in the current literature. Research methods included collecting and analyzing student work, audio field notes, class transcripts, and both individual and focus group interviews. In addition, the collected data was analyzed by diverse networks of teacher researchers at both a local and national level, thereby bringing multiple perspectives to the analysis. Focused around the following question—what does it mean for a teacher and students to take a critical stance on language—this study concerns itself with the roles which were played, the topics and issues which were raised, the ways in which knowledge was generated, and the range of student attitudes on critical language issues. (Fecho, 1995, p. 2)

Although this is a study of Fecho's classroom and the interactions that occur around language use, he also owns his own role as insider, turning it to his advantage by arguing that it provides a rare emic perspective on classroom life, while also incorporating rigorous ethnographic methods and data analysis.

Insider in Collaboration With Other Insiders

Insider researchers often collaborate with other insiders as a way to do research that not only might have a greater impact on the setting, but is also more democratic. However, power relations in a setting operate even when insiders think they are being collaborative. For instance, while principals, teachers, and counselors may collaborate as insiders in a school located in a low-income community, they may or may not view the students or community as part of the collaboration. Unless they do, the results of their action research might benefit them at the expense of the powerless. This is also true of outside change agents who collaborate with schools or other organizations. In such cases, what may look like collaboration can end up being unintended collusion by professionals against the interests of their clients and communities (Anderson, 1999). This is especially true when outsiders are invited in by those at the top of the organizational or community hierarchy. These issues of power become increasingly important as funded participatory international development projects are led by researchers from so-called developed nations working in developing nations (Chambers, 1997).

These insider collaborations—the second category in Table 3.1—are manifested in many organizations as inquiry groups that go under different names. In business, they are often teams that engage in what is called data-based decision making. In communities, they can be Alinsky-inspired, interfaith community organizing groups such as the Industrial Areas Foundation (IAF), parent organizations in schools, or consumer groups. In education, they go under names such as teacher study groups, teacher inquiry groups, critical friends groups, or leadership teams.

These various forms of insider collaborative inquiry vary in their degree of autonomy. Some groups are fairly spontaneous and work at the margins of organizations or communities (see Miller, 1990), whereas others either evolve into or are incorporated into the governance structure (Johnson, 2002). Collaborative inquiry groups often are convened by formal institutional efforts that create site-based management teams to engage in data-driven organizational change efforts. While more autonomous groups provide more freedom and idiosyncrasy, more mainstream groups hold out more possibility of impacting the overall organizational culture. Some argue that autonomous inquiry groups lead to greater balkanization and micropolitics (Holly, 1989); others argue that groups that are brought into the organizational mainstream may be too easily co-opted (Herr, 1999a; Maguire, 1987b; Miller, 1990). Regardless of how groups of participants interested in inquiry choose to situate themselves along the continuum of formal institutional to informal autonomous, these group efforts have several aspects in common: they engage in inquiry in ways that help the group move from working as isolated individuals toward a collaborative community; they seek to engage their members in learning and change; they work toward influencing organizational change; and they offer opportunities for personal, professional, and institutional transformation.[4]

Headman (1992), a fourth-grade teacher, did a collaborative study for her dissertation with the parents of her students.

> Parents and teachers typically establish and maintain hierarchical relationships which ascribe excessive authority to the school, thus limiting the possibilities for dialogue and mutual learning. Their discussions of children's literacy often fail to acknowledge the contributions that parents can make, based on their knowledge and experiences with children at home. Neglecting parents' voices in schools, and in home and school literacy research, means the parents' critical role in supporting children's literacy development is overlooked. By investigating with parents their perspectives on children's literacy experiences in and out of school, this study seeks to understand the relationships between children's home and school literacy and to model processes by which parents and teachers develop a reciprocal dialogue. Eight parents of my fourth grade public school students joined me in a two-month co-investigation. Individually and collectively we raised questions, observed, documented, and reflected on children's uses of reading and writing in and out of school. Weekly meetings were held with individual families and occasionally involved all participants. Data sources included literacy diaries written by parents and myself about children's experiences, audiotapes of meetings, participants' reflective journal entries, and children's literacy profiles constructed jointly by parents and the teacher. The study's findings provide evidence that parents can be a rich resource to teachers and researchers. When parents documented children's literacy experiences at home, they observed a wide variety that were not school-like or school-directed. The data reveal patterns of participation and learning from literacy activities that distinguish families from one another and from their children's shared school experiences. This suggests that organizing literacy interactions in classrooms or homes after a single model would be inappropriate. Through the parent teacher research process, parents raised issues about current practices in classroom grouping, integrative curriculum, assessment, and teaching and learning relationships, providing further evidence for the importance of including parents' knowledge and experience in the design of effective learning contexts for their children. These findings suggest that beyond routine parent conferences, alternative structures for dialogue with teachers are needed that allow for parents' critical reflection and substantive contributions to the school literacy curriculum. (Headman, 1992, p. 7)

Insider(s) in Collaboration With Outsider(s)

A less common position is insiders initiating collaborations with outsiders. In such cases, organizational or community members contract or invite outsiders to collaborate on research. This collaboration can also range from merely bringing someone in to consult on methodology to collaborations that involve outsiders from the point of problem definition. Collaborative or participatory action research (PAR) in general raises unique issues with regard to how knowledge claims are justified and how power and control over the research process is distributed.

PAR: Reciprocal Collaboration (Insider-Outsider Teams)

If there were an ideal form of PAR, the insider-outsider team would probably fit the bill. However, because all action research is done within a particular context, there may be many situations in which this would not be the best way to design a study—at least not initially. Furthermore, achieving this kind of reciprocal collaboration often requires many years of negotiation among all stakeholders, as illustrated in Lynn Mock's dissertation study described in chapter 6. After years of engaging in action research in organizational contexts, Whyte (1991) concluded that

> the social scientist should not seek to establish such a partnership the moment he or she enters the field. In industry or agriculture, the technical specialists will generally have little understanding of what the social scientist might contribute, and they will react against the newcomer who claims powers they lack. Those social scientists most successful in establishing such interdisciplinary partnerships view themselves initially as participant observers, showing respect for the work of practitioners and technical specialists, and seeking to learn from them. As the social scientist gains an understanding of the organizational culture and work systems, he or she will find ways of contributing that are appreciated by the technical specialists. This will pave the way for establishing the full partnerships represented by PAR. (p. 240)

While this may be the ideal for a PAR study, in practical terms, a doctoral student may not have the time for this kind of full partnership to form, unless it forms as part of a pilot study, or, as in Mock's case, previous to her entering the study. In the following section, we will further address problems associated with arriving at the right level of participation among researchers and participants.

PAR: Outsider(s) in Collaboration With Insider(s)

The notion of insider and outsider is often a matter of degree. On the continuum of positionality in Table 3.1, positions 4, 5, and 6 illustrate the gradations from participatory insider-outsider teams all the way to nonparticipatory outsider research. For instance, in the studies described in chapter 6, the Mock (1999) study was part of a collaboration that would be located near 4, the middle of the continuum. The McIntyre (1995) study would be located closer to 5 on the continuum. This probably is the most common type of collaborative action research because it is more common for outsiders to initiate research projects than insiders, except perhaps when insiders invite outsiders in to do a collaborative evaluation (which was the case in the Mock study).

Those projects that locate themselves at the center of the continuum of positionality in Table 3.1 are rare indeed. As our case examples in chapter 6 suggest, insiders are often too busy to be full participants, and seldom do the incentive structures of organizations—other than universities—reward research. While the Mock (1999) collaborative study described in chapter 6 came perhaps as close as is possible to creating an insider-outsider team (Bartunek & Louis, 1996), even these researchers acknowledged the difficulty of negotiating equal levels of commitment to the project (Kelly et al., 2004).

Cochran-Smith and Lytle (1993) point out that there is some justifiable fear that collaborations between university researchers and practitioners or communities can be co-opted by the university researchers, who have greater incentives and interest in publication. Whyte's (1991) insight, mentioned previously, about the defensiveness of organizational insiders goes a long way in explaining why they are often reluctant to invite outsiders into their research projects. For instance, the Teachers-as-Researchers Special Interest Group of the American Educational Research Association initially discouraged academics from joining so they could have conversations that were not monopolized by university scholars.

The issue of what each stakeholder wants out of the research needs to be negotiated carefully if reciprocity is to be achieved. The attitude of PAR can be illustrated by a model reported by Tolley and Bentley (1996), which is adapted by MYRADA, a nongovernmental organization involved in rural development in India, from the four squares of self-knowledge published in Luft (1963; see Table 3.2). When outsiders enter a collaborative research study with the mindset of the third quadrant of this diagram, they frame themselves as outside

Table 3.2   The Four Squares of Knowledge

I We know They know	II We don't know They know
III We know They don't know	IV We don't know They don't know

Table 3.3   Participatory Methods: Means to What End?

Mode of Participation	Involvement of Local People	Relationship of Research and Action to Local People
Co-option	Token; representatives are chosen, but no real input or power	on
Compliance	Tasks are assigned, with incentives; outsiders decide agenda	for
Consultation	Local opinions asked, outsiders analyze and decide on a course of action	for/with
Cooperation	Local people work together with outsiders to determine priorities; responsibility remains with outsiders for directing the process	with
Colearning	Local people and outsiders share their knowledge to create new understanding and work together to form action plans, with outsider facilitation	with/by
Collective action	Local people set their own agenda and mobilize to carry it out in the absence of outside initiators and facilitators	by

experts rather than collaborative researchers. This often reinforces a tendency by insiders to place themselves in quadrant II, undervaluing their own professional or vernacular knowledge (McLaughlin, 1996). The goal of collaborative research is to reduce the tendencies of quadrants II and III and to expand quadrant I.

Issues of reciprocity for PAR and collaborative research are very complex. Cornwall (1996) has adapted a continuum of purposes for PAR that is displayed in Table 3.3. She provides a useful list of the varying degrees of participation/collaboration that take place in PAR.

For excellent discussions of reflexivity and the external researcher in PAR, see Dickson (1997), Dickson and Green (2001), and Maguire (1987b). Bartunek and Louis (1996) provide a more extended discussion of when insider-outsider teams are appropriate and what makes them successful.

Often it is difficult to identify a researcher's position, and thus the issue of whether one is actually doing action research may be called into question. The following dissertation abstract provides an example in which the researcher's position is ambiguous. She is a facilitator of several teacher research groups, works for the school district, but is an outsider to the teachers' professional settings. Her working hypothesis is that teacher research groups, if left on their own, tend to reproduce current practices rather than challenge them. She highlights the importance of the facilitator, but her positionality as a member of the district hierarchy implies a particular agenda.

> The purpose of this research study is to examine my four-year role as a facilitator of twelve teacher research groups throughout British Columbia. I examine facilitated teacher research groups as one pathway to engendering educational reform. My thesis is that, without the external voice of the facilitator, contexts for pedagogical dialogue have the possibility of becoming nothing more than a retelling of incidents that occur consistently in the dailiness of teaching. Without the external facilitator, teacher research groups may become rooted in process at the expense of substance. The rigorous conversations and the rethinking of practice may be in jeopardy of being replaced by sessions in which teachers are emotionally and socially supported, yet changes in practice are not viewed as vital. This research study focuses on problematic aspects, tensions, and perplexing questions that emerged in my practice as a facilitator for teacher research groups. These dilemmas included grappling with the colleague/expert dichotomy, "contrived" collegiality, unexamined practitioner constructions of knowledge, and prodding practitioners to move beyond the seductive peril of retelling their own stories to take action towards rethinking and subsequently changing their own practice. Teachers viewed my role as facilitator as important because it contributed an external perspective which focused practitioners on what made a difference to student learning. (Dockendorf, 1995, p. 3)

Positionality occurs not only in terms of inside/outside, but also in terms of one's position in the organizational or social hierarchy, and one's position of power vis-à-vis other stakeholders inside and outside the setting. As we will discuss below, all of these nuances must be taken into account in an action research dissertation.

Outsider(s) Studies Insider(s)

This category may seem irrelevant to action research because it describes a traditional outsider position taken by quantitative and qualitative researchers. However, this end of the continuum does contain some gradations of insider-outsider collaborations and some interesting debates about whether action research is really that different from traditional research. In this section we will discuss (a) how action research is different from what social scientists call *applied research;* (b) collaborative research among outsiders; (c) research done by outsiders who study action research projects; and (d) scholarly work on action research as a methodology (its history, epistemology, etc.).

There is some debate about whether action research is a separate epistemology or merely a type of applied social science research. Spjelkavik (1999) states,

> The difference between the applied research model and the action research model is that participation with the actors in the field is an important part of action research. . . . Although the applied research model is very general, it is no different epistemologically from an action research model. Action research is simply one of several possible ways to conduct applied research. . . . Thus, action research is a method that can be fruitfully combined with other methods (questionnaires, interviews, observations, whatever), and in this respect it does not require specific epistemological commitments. (p. 126)

He sees the participatory aspect of action research as merely supplementing the applied model. Thus, an action research study on this end of the continuum is viewed as applied research in which the outsider may engage more closely with the study's participants. This level of engagement, according to Spjelkavik (1999), can vary during the life of the study. In his study of Norwegian fish farms, he began as an outsider doing applied research aimed at generating knowledge about rural development and survival strategies in marginal or remote areas. The study evolved into PAR as the questions shifted and as relationships with informants deepened.

Ethnographers have traditionally lived in their informants' communities and have called what they do *participant observation.* In fact, the ability to participate effectively in community life is often a sign that the ethnographer has learned the culture. Nevertheless, few ethnographers would call what they do PAR. Thus, the notion of *outsider* is complex and nuanced. In fact, just as insiders collaborate with other insiders to do action research projects, outsiders sometimes collaborate with other outsiders to form collaborative research teams. They are not necessarily doing action research, but they are doing research collaboratively. When doing any kind of applied research with participants, it is difficult to predict how a study will evolve in terms of its action orientation or the extent to which participants are included in deliberations about questions, methods, data gathering, findings, and dissemination of the research.

Because action research has gained popularity in recent years, there are a large number of doctoral students who have studied action research projects but are not using action research to do so. Most of these are qualitative or mixed methods studies of teacher research teams in schools or international development projects. Although these are not action research dissertations and thus not the focus of this book, it is important to emphasize that action research projects can be documented by insiders, outsiders, or PAR teams.

For instance, O'Donnell-Allen (1999) did a study for her dissertation of a teacher research group, but positioned herself as an outsider. She makes no pretense of doing collaborative research of any kind. Her goal was to observe the group and gather examples of teacher discourse. It is an example of a study *of* teacher research rather than a study *with* teacher researchers.

Besides outsider research *on* action research projects, there is also scholarship on action research methods and epistemology. These dissertations use a combination of historical, philosophical, or sociological methods. Noffke (1990), who has published extensively on action research since her dissertation, did a conceptual analysis of action research, asking the following questions central to understanding and evaluating action research:

> 1) Under what conditions does it emerge as a competing form of research? 2) How do forms and intentions of action research vary? And 3) What forms of action research offer a possibility for educational research that is responsive to teachers' working conditions, to theory, and to the furtherance of social justice? (p. 4)

Using primarily historical methods and feminist theory, she found— among other findings—contradictions in action research between democratic and social engineering intentions and methods.

Zuniga-Urrutia (1992), who herself did action research in Chile in the 1970s, interviewed 31 action researchers, not "to define what 'true' or 'real' action research was, but to construct a conceptual framework to facilitate dialogue about issues and differences in action research practice" (p. 2). Like Noffke (1990), she found that views of action researchers varied from

> a "restricted" view which is micro-based and emphasizes social efficiency and traditional research; a "broad" view which is macro-oriented and emphasizes empowerment and social action; and a mixed view which attempts to integrate aspects of each of these approaches. (p. 3)

We have further discussed these views of action research in chapter 2, drawing on what Habermas (1971) called the knowledge interests behind different types of action research.

Multiple Positionalities

In this chapter, we have attempted to help action researchers clarify their often-complex relationships to the setting that is being studied. There are other ways, however, to think about researcher positionality. The list below provides multiple ways of thinking about one's position within an action research project and some citations of work that can help sort these issues out.

1. Insider/Outsider positionality vis-à-vis the setting under study (Anderson & Herr, 1999; Cochran-Smith & Lytle, 1993).

2. Hierarchical position or level of informal power within the organization/ community (Anderson & Jones, 2000; Israel et al., 2003).

3. Position vis-à-vis dominant groups in society—class, race, ethnicity, gender, sexual orientation, age, ability/disability, religion, and so forth (Anzaldua, 1987; Bell, 2001; Collins, 1990).

4. Position within colonial relations within and between nation states (Chambers, 1997; Tuhiwai Smith, 1999; Villenas, 1996; Willinsky, 2000).

The complexity of the notion of inside/outside is captured by Collins's (1990) discussion of being an "outsider-within." She suggests that one's location in an organization or community makes for varying vantage points and differing lenses of "reality." Some people are outsiders-within, residing in the margins and observing "the contradictions between the dominant group's actions and ideologies" (p. 11). Collins maintains that outsiders-within offer a specialized, subjugated knowledge, a "peculiar marginality," that provides a unique standpoint on self and society. For example, women in a male-dominated organization may become expert observers of the male culture as they navigate their day-to-day interactions with colleagues. The knowledge they possess in this case is not unlike that of Collins's example of black slaves who have "special knowledge" of the white household because their survival is dependent on knowing the culture of whites. The dominant group is under no equivalent obligation. As Foucault (1980) points out, subjugated knowledge is offered by those who are sufficiently outside the mainstream of an organization or entity, perhaps those located down low on the institutional hierarchy. This specialized knowledge can foster organizational learning or be seen as a threat to the maintenance of the culture of an institution.

But each of us as researchers occupies multiple positions that intersect and may bring us into conflicting allegiances or alliances within our research sites. We may occupy positions where we are included as insiders while simultaneously, in some dimensions, we identify as outsiders. In the latter case, these dimensions often encompass one's race, social class, gender, or sexual orientation in relationship to the site being studied. These dimensions extend into the worldview that one brings to the institution, both in terms of political or ideological beliefs as well as cultural assumptions. Each of these dimensions enters into the construction of the reality we capture in our research. We suggest that our obligation as researchers is to interrogate our multiple positionalities in relationship to the question under study. Our sense is that, in making explicit the tensions we experience as researchers in our varying roles and statuses, we have the possibility of crafting uniquely complex understandings of the research question. In addition, we hope to avoid the blind spots that come with unexamined beliefs.

Tammy Ann Schwartz's (2002) dissertation research exemplifies the complexities of positionality. Schwartz was a doctoral student at the University of

Cincinnati who did a PAR project with 11 urban Appalachian girls to explore their writing practices.

> After dialoguing about writing and related issues, the girls conducted their investigation by interviewing their sisters, mothers and female friends and cousins. Themes of place, identity, class and writing emerged from subsequent analysis and dialogues. These dialogues, in turn, led to action as the girls began to confront class-specific stereotypes connected to place. (p. 2)

On the surface, Schwartz appears to be an outsider convening group dialogues with these girls in a classic PAR model. Her adult status and educational level also make her an outsider to the girls. However, Schwartz is also an insider in terms of her working-class origins, which matches that of the girls, but, more important, it turns out she also grew up in a neighborhood adjacent to the one in which these girls live.

> What follows is a story of lives and research. For me, it is a story of traveling away from the community, traveling back, traveling between knowing and not knowing, between insider and outsider. For the girls, it is a story of traveling between knowing and conscientization and action, and between living and revising neighborhood narratives about what it means to be a girl in this place at this time. For all of us together, it is a story of questioning our selves, our neighborhood, our identities, our worlds. (p. 12)

We share her introductory narrative below in part as an example of how researchers can narrate themselves into their dissertations, but also to demonstrate the tensions that arise when one shares certain positionalities with one's participants.

> I am home again, indeed, and it is this research that brings me home. It brings me back to my days as a young urban Appalachian girl growing up in a "bad" neighborhood full of "hillbillies" and "white trash." Willingly, I assumed the shame so often associated with my neighborhood, a shame outsiders expected me to claim. "Oh, you are from City Hill?" they would say with disdain. I also heard what they didn't say. "You are no good if you are from that neighborhood, that place." "Well, they must be right," I thought. Of course, they were right. After all, they were better dressed than me, they didn't use no double negatives, they had their own washers, and they didn't have to ride the bus—they owned cars. Different, I was . . . from them.
> Who I was, according to so many "others," was associated with where I lived, City Hill. Trash on the streets, crowded Laundromats, corner convenience stores good for pops, bags of chips, and rolls of toilet paper when the big grocery store five blocks up the Avenue felt too far away. Section-eight housing, food stamps, Mom's welfare check, roaches in the kitchen, no child support for my mother, trips to the local Goodwill for "new" sweaters, and lots of love, hard work and a stubbornness to be somebody. I wanted out. Out was the only way to claim an identity as

someone—at least as someone who mattered in ways that gave one access to power. In my adolescent eyes, getting an education could get me out. There were problems with this "education-gettin'," though. Education-gettin' meant I might not talk like my family, I might move away and become part of a foreign and scary world. Sometimes, accepting my "white trashness" was simple and comforting. I knew the expectations.

Now, more than twenty years and lots of education-gettin' later, it is ironic that what I used to escape, education that is, is what brings me back to the place I longed to flee, the place that filled me with shame to call home—City Hill. I am home again, indeed, and it is haunting.

The research presented in this dissertation takes me back to my youth by taking me back to a neighborhood similar and adjacent to the one in which I grew up. It also takes me back to my adolescent self. Because of this work I am reminded of struggles I encountered growing up, struggles that I can only now name as ones related to my class—poor, my race—white, my gender—female, and my ethnicity—Appalachian, and the strange and mysterious ways in which all of these identities intersected with place—my neighborhood. (pp. 6–7)

Rivera (1999) did a similar PAR study with six Puerto Rican and Dominican young women. She studied their strategies of resistance for self-determination and collective determination within various relationships and contexts, including their schools, neighborhoods, and homes. She found that forms of resistance varied by setting and were often simultaneously oppressive and liberating. She explored resistance patterns by engaging with the young women in three participatory projects over 2 years: a community video project, an arts-centered project on Latinas' lives, and an educational workshop series. Rivera found that participatory methods were instrumental in developing relationships with the women and maintaining the integrity of the study.

An Appalachian woman studying Appalachian girls or a Latina woman studying Latina young women provides a certain insider status and deep tacit knowledge about the participants' ethnic communities and gendered perspectives. There is also an added sense of self-discovery and social advocacy for the researchers. However, being an insider in any sense also brings a subtle tendency to take some aspects of the setting for granted and a need to make the apparently familiar seem strange.

The Outsider-Within Stance as a Flawed Approach to Action Research

While Collins (1990) and others have discussed the special vantage point that being a marginalized member of society—an outsider within—provides, there is another way that action researchers—particularly practitioners—use an outsider-within approach that is dishonest and tends to skew the research process.

Too often, when insiders to an organization or community do dissertation research, the researcher and the dissertation committee members treat it as outsider research. Often, they simply draw on the validity criteria for more traditional forms of research and ignore the insider status of the researcher. In such cases, insiders end up taking an outsider-within stance in which they frame the study inappropriately, using outsider validity criteria (e.g., prolonged engagement with the field) that fails to address the unique dilemmas of practitioners studying their own sites.

This most often occurs when members higher up in the organizational hierarchy engage in action research and when neither the doctoral student nor the dissertation committee have familiarized themselves with the tenets of action research. We believe that this outsider-within stance toward practitioner research causes epistemological and methodological problems, since validity criteria—particularly for qualitative research—was designed with outsiders in mind. The dilemma of the insider is the opposite of that of the outsider:

> Academics (outsiders) want to understand what it is like to be an insider without "going native" and losing the outsider's perspective. Practitioners (insiders) already know what it is like to be an insider, but because they are "native" to the setting, they must work to see the taken-for-granted aspects of their practice from an outsider's perspective. (Anderson, Herr, & Nihlen, 1994, p. 27)

The outsider-within position also ignores the potential of studying the researcher/practitioner's ongoing actions and shifting perceptions within the setting as part of the research. Instead, following the norms of outsider research, one's actions within the setting are either not acknowledged or seen as a problem of reactivity or contamination of the setting. Such a position is part of a research tradition that sees the sole purpose of the research as generating valid knowledge as a contribution to a knowledge base in a particular field. Anderson and Jones (2000), in their study of practitioner research dissertations, found that "although personal, professional, or organization/social transformation might be a byproduct of insiders doing 'outsider within' research, it was usually reported—if at all—as an afterthought in the dissertations" (p. 440).

To downplay or fail to acknowledge one's insider status is deceptive and allows the researcher to avoid the kind of intense self-reflection that is the hallmark of good practitioner research. Such deceptive studies are often done for the sake of convenience or to use an evaluation of a local program as a dissertation study. Anderson and Jones (2000) found that when researchers authentically positioned themselves as insiders doing action research or self-studies, they moved individual, organizational, and social transformation through actions taken within the setting to the forefront. These authentic studies were more likely to engage in the traditional action research spiral of iterative cycles of plan-act-observe-reflect (Lewin, 1948). The increased understandings of practice and the practice setting that result from these studies represent the "findings" of this type of self-reflective research.

Conclusion

Our purpose in this chapter is not to recommend any particular positionality as an ideal. Although it is true that position 4 on the continuum in Table 3.1 (the insider-outsider team) represents the most potentially democratic approach, we believe that knowledge production from all positions is valid as long as one is honest and reflective about one's multiple positionalities. As we have argued, self-reflection has important consequences for the study's trustworthiness and on the ethics of the research. In the following chapter, we will discuss in more detail how positionality determines how one thinks about the criteria for quality or trustworthiness of the study. Insiders, outsiders, and insider-outsider teams all have different dilemmas to resolve in designing and carrying out an action research project. For students doing action research dissertations, it is crucial to think these issues through prior to beginning the study, and to make them explicit in the dissertation proposal.

4

Quality Criteria
for Action Research

An Ongoing Conversation

*Q*uality, *goodness, validity, trustworthiness, credibility,* and *workability* have all been suggested as terms to describe criteria for good action research. Positivists have tended to prefer *validity* (Campbell & Stanley, 1963) and naturalistic researchers have preferred *trustworthiness* (Lincoln & Guba, 1985). Neither term is adequate for action research because neither acknowledges its *action-oriented* outcomes. Action researchers, like all researchers, are interested in whether knowledge generated from the research is valid or trustworthy, but they are usually also interested in outcomes that go beyond knowledge generation.

Rather than coin a new term for indicators of quality, we have preferred to use *validity* with qualifying adjectives, for reasons we will discuss below. However, the terminology one chooses to describe the methodology of a dissertation will depend on the extent to which the research must be legitimated to a dissertation committee. So the choice of terms is ultimately a political decision. Patricia Maguire did a PAR dissertation in 1987 at the University of Massachusetts, and we highly recommend her advice to graduate students:

> By way of advice to others I'd say try to head off some of the academic disappointments by being careful and deliberate about the dissertation committee you put together if, like I did, you have control of it. Seek out faculty promoting, or at least open to, alternative paradigm research approaches. The ideal is to find faculty as open to learning with you as they are to teaching you. (Maguire, 1993, p. 175)

Because action research is not mainstream research in universities, it is often necessary to defend it as a legitimate form of research for a dissertation. This will largely depend on how sympathetic and knowledgeable committee members are, so Patricia Maguire's advice to select a committee carefully is crucial to successfully defending the research. Making good decisions at the point of selecting a dissertation committee can determine whether the dissertation process is exciting and energizing or highly frustrating.

Some committees will assume the research is legitimate and not require an extensive espistemological discussion defending the methodology itself. However, even if you needn't defend action research as a legitimate research methodology, you will need to defend the specifics of the particular decisions you have made throughout your study. This will require understanding how quality criteria for action research differ from quality criteria for a traditional quantitative or qualitative study.

We use the term *validity* in this chapter not because we wish to adopt positivistic language for action research, but because doctoral students are usually introduced to this language in their research courses. *Internal validity* is generally defined as the trustworthiness of inferences drawn from data. *External validity* refers to how well these inferences generalize to a larger population or are transferable to other contexts. Because most academic researchers are part of a positivistic tradition inherited from the natural and physical sciences, they consider the notion of validity to be of utmost importance in all research. The more recent influence of ethnography and qualitative case study methods has tempered this tendency somewhat and put forth new ways of thinking about validity. Since qualitative researchers have developed their own set of rules about the validity of qualitative research findings, we will review these rules before proposing new ones for action research.

Although qualitative researchers are not in total agreement, they generally reject the claims of positivism that the best research is fundamentally about pursuing *truth value* (internal validity) by demonstrating that causes and their effects have been isolated. Lincoln and Guba (1985) have proposed that the comparable standard of *trustworthiness* is more appropriate for naturalistic or qualitative inquiry. According to Lincoln and Guba, a study's trustworthiness involves the demonstration that the researcher's interpretations of the data are credible, or "ring true," to those who provided the data.

Although the standards for qualitative inquiry are different from those used by quantitative researchers, they still may not be appropriate for action researchers. Most qualitative researchers want to study a phenomenon in its natural setting—thus the term *naturalistic inquiry*. To the extent that researchers act within or change a setting through their presence, they "contaminate" the setting. Though somewhat overstated, a qualitative researcher wants to be a fly on the wall, observing a social setting as it develops independent of the researcher. While it is true that traditional ethnographers often lived in the communities they studied, had key informants, and interacted with participants in order to gain access to the setting and to gain their trust, the basic position of outsider is intentionally maintained.

As one moves along the continuum of positionality in chapter 3 from outsider to insider, the relationship of the researcher to the setting begins to shift. When an insider to the setting (e.g., a social worker in an agency, a nurse in a hospital, a teacher in a school) is also the researcher, the dilemmas experienced are the opposite of those the outsider experiences. Academics (outsiders) want to understand what it is like to be an insider without "going native" and losing the outsider's perspective. Practitioners, because they *are* "native" to the setting, must work to see the taken-for-granted aspects of their practice from an outsider perspective. This is further complicated by the fact that many academic researchers have, in fact, been practitioners and are, therefore, in some sense both insiders and outsiders. Moreover, many practitioners have been socialized into academic research through graduate study and have internalized many outsider social categories. Therefore, the distance between university researchers and practitioners is sometimes not as great as we make out in theory.

For researchers who are positioned as outsiders, but want to engage in participatory action research (PAR), the dilemmas will depend on the extent to which the participants are merely helping out with the research or whether they are true partners in the research. To the extent that a true partnership exists, the action researcher over time begins to take an insider perspective.

Qualitative researchers often disagree among themselves about the purposes of research and criteria for validity. For example, some qualitative researchers prefer a more interventionist, emancipatory approach to qualitative research. Because of the more traditional qualitative researcher's fly-on-the-wall approach to the research setting, some critical and feminist researchers claim that qualitative research is still mired in positivism, in that it "affirms a social world that is meant to be gazed upon but not challenged or transformed" (Roman, 1992, p. 573).

Furthermore, many qualitative researchers (and most action researchers) still see the social sciences as the model for what they consider data, or evidence, for assertions. This usually involves some form of observation, interview, survey, or archival/document analysis methods. More narrative types of qualitative and action research drawing from the humanities are often viewed with suspicion. While we have addressed these humanities-oriented approaches to some extent throughout this book, we recommend further reading in this area if you think such an approach will better capture your findings (see Barone, 2000; Connelly & Clandinin, 1990; Eisner, 1997; Evans, 1995).

Delegitimizing Action Research: Opposition in the Academy

Academics tend to be comfortable with action research as a form of local knowledge that leads to change within the practice setting itself, but are less comfortable when it is presented as public knowledge with epistemic claims beyond the practice setting. This is particularly important in the case of dissertations, whose primary justification is the production of new knowledge. A recent debate in the field of education helps to illustrate some of these arguments being used against action research as a legitimate form of academic inquiry. Many of the arguments are focused more on practitioner research, or the notion of insider practitioners generating knowledge, largely unmediated by academic researchers. However, it is clear that what bothers many academics is also the type of knowledge that is generated—knowledge that in many cases is practice-driven rather than theory-driven.

For example, Huberman (1996) criticizes Cochran-Smith and Lytle (1993), Miller (1990), Gallas (1993), and others who defend action research done by teachers as guilty of hubris because of what he considers exaggerated claims for teacher research. For many academics, the acceptance of action research is given only on the condition that a separate category of knowledge be created for it. This is usually expressed as some variation on formal (created in universities) knowledge versus practical (created in practice settings) knowledge and a strict separation of research from practice (Fenstermacher, 1994; Hammack, 1997; Huberman, 1996; Richardson, 1994; Wong, 1995a, 1995b). For example, Richardson (1994) defines action research as "practical inquiry" which focuses on the "improvement of practice" and then uses her own definition to relegate it to secondary status vis-à-vis formal (read "real") research. Fenstermacher (1994) declares that practical knowledge results from participating in and reflecting on action and experience; is bounded by the situation or context in which it arises; may or may not be capable of immediate expression in speech or writing; and deals with "how to do things, the right place and time to do them, or how to see and interpret events related to one's actions" (p. 12).

In response, Cochran-Smith and Lytle (1998) reject the formal/practical knowledge dualism as unhelpful and see it as greatly limiting the very nature of teaching and teacher research, which they claim is more about

> how teachers' actions are infused with complex and multi-layered understandings of learners, culture, class, gender, literacy, social issues, institutions, communities, materials, texts, and curricula. It is about how teachers work together to develop and alter their questions and interpretive frameworks informed not only by thoughtful consideration of the immediate situation and the particular students they teach and have taught but also by the multiple contexts—social, political, historical, and cultural—within which they work. (p. 24)

Moreover, Clandinin and Connelly (1995) have argued that outsider knowledge is often experienced by practitioners as a "rhetoric of conclusions," which enters the practitioners' professional landscape through informational conduits that funnel propositional and theoretical knowledge to them with little understanding that their landscape is personal, contextual, subjective, temporal, historical, and relational among people. Clearly, the formal/practical knowledge debate is about more than research epistemology and methodology; it is about the very nature of professional practice itself and what types of knowledge can best inform it.

Such a dualistic approach to the insider-outsider conundrum is partly solved by participatory action researchers, who suggest that when research is done collaboratively, it brings both the insider and outsider perspectives into the research. Nevertheless, those who approach research from a strictly academic perspective will still want to know how data is collaboratively analyzed and how findings are negotiated. For many academics, this may sound too much like research findings by committee. (See chapter 6 for an example of this type of collaboration.)

While the notions of insider and outsider research are useful in calling attention to the unique problems entailed in each, neither have a monopoly on knowledge. While practitioners have a wealth of tacit knowledge and are what Geertz calls more "experience-near" to the everyday life of organizations, they do not have privileged access to truth. As Carter (1993) argues, practitioners' accounts of their reality are themselves constructions of reality and not reality itself. We cannot escape the basic problems of knowledge generation by elevating practitioners' accounts of practice to a privileged status. This is why collaborative and participatory forms of research among insiders and outsiders hold so much promise.

Redefining Rigor: Criteria of Quality for Action Research

Early naturalistic researchers insisted on their own validity criteria separate from that of Campbell and Stanley (1963), because they felt their work would be unfairly evaluated by others' criteria. We likewise suggest that action research should not be judged by the same validity criteria with which we judge positivistic and naturalistic research. This is not to say that there is no overlap or that it is less rigorous, but that a new definition of rigor is required that does not mislead or marginalize action researchers. As action research is disseminated beyond local sites, we believe, there is a need to deepen conversations about these issues. One can legitimately ask, If we can't use current validity criteria to evaluate action research, how *do* we evaluate it? How do we distinguish "good" action research from "poor"? Most important, who should develop these criteria?

We first began to struggle with these issues in the late 1980s when coauthor Herr embarked on action research in the middle school in which she worked as a counselor and teacher. Steeped in qualitative research learned in graduate school, it was the tension of trying to apply that same methodology in her own site that brought us into an ongoing conversation about action research. With both of us now in academic settings, we have had the opportunity to continue the dialogue with practitioners when we teach action research. In fact, it was this dual perspective of both university and practice cultures that caused us to perceive the problems we describe in this book.

Still, the notion of academics—even sympathetic ones—defining criteria for practitioners is fraught with problems. Furthermore, as discussed in chapter 2, action research is a cover term for multiple traditions. Validity criteria are somewhat different for more outsider-oriented action research than that which is insider-oriented. Methodologically, the criteria offered below were developed through the interrogation of Herr's middle school action research in dialogue with established research criteria; they are based on our own experiences as action researchers, our work with others, and a search of existing work on this topic. In the ensuing years, we have noticed that others have attempted to define indicators of quality for action research, and we discuss those as well.

We have addressed these issues of validity for action research elsewhere (Anderson & Herr, 1999; Anderson, Herr & Nihlen, 1994), and they have been summarized in Gall, Gall and Borg (2003) and Mills (2000). Our goal in disseminating these criteria is not to close down the conversation, but rather to open it up to dialogue with both academics and practitioners. It is too soon to formulate criteria for quality in the absence of significant dialogue and in the context of multiple approaches to action research.

Our validity criteria are tentative and meant to democratize action research, cautioning against a narrow insider or outsider view of the problematic situation under study. On the other hand, for the student doing a dissertation, a set of criteria that are widely cited and summarized in mainstream research texts may provide the legitimation needed to get a dissertation through a less than totally sympathetic dissertation committee. We offer these validity criteria here as an invitation to other action researchers and academics to sustain a dialogue regarding these issues across the whole continuum of action research.

We have linked our five validity criteria (outcome, process, democratic, catalytic, and dialogic) to the goals of action research. Most traditions of action research agree on the following goals: (a) the generation of new knowledge, (b) the achievement of action-oriented outcomes, (c) the education of both researcher and participants, (d) results that are relevant to the local setting, and (e) a sound and appropriate research methodology. Based on these goals, we have identified indicators of quality for action research studies. In Table 4.1 we show how these goals are linked to validity criteria.

Table 4.1   Anderson and Herr's Goals of Action Research and Validity Criteria

Goals of Action Research	Quality/Validity Criteria
1) The generation of new knowledge	Dialogic and process validity
2) The achievement of action-oriented outcomes	Outcome validity
3) The education of both researcher and participants	Catalytic validity
4) Results that are relevant to the local setting	Democratic validity
5) A sound and appropriate research methodology	Process validity

Outcome Validity. One test of the validity of action research is the extent to which actions occur, which leads to a resolution of the problem that led to the study. Greenwood and Levin (1998) call this criteria "workability" and link it to John Dewey's notion of pragmatism. Watkins (1991) points out that "many Action Research studies abort at the stage of diagnosis of a problem or the implementation of a single solution strategy, irrespective of whether or not it resolves the presenting problem" (p. 8). Brooks and Watkins (1994) suggest *skillfulness* as action research's equivalent to *credibility* for naturalistic inquiry or *validity* for positivist research. Action researchers must be competent at both research procedures and moving participants toward successful action outcomes.

Jacobson (1998) uses the term *integrity* to discuss his criteria for good action research. Integrity must rest on "the quality of action which emerges from it, and the quality of data on which the action is based" (p. 130). Thus, outcome validity is synonymous with the "successful" outcome of the research project. This, of course, begs the question raised below under democratic validity, that is, successful for whom? Outcome validity also acknowledges the fact that rigorous action research, rather than simply solving a problem, forces the researcher to reframe the problem in a more complex way, often leading to a new set of questions or problems. This ongoing reframing of problems leads to the spiraling dynamic that characterizes the process of most action research over a sustained period of inquiry.

Process validity asks to what extent problems are framed and solved in a manner that permits ongoing learning of the individual or system. In this sense, outcome validity is dependent on process validity in that, if the process is superficial or flawed, the outcome will reflect it. Are the "findings" a result of a series of reflective cycles that include the ongoing problematization of the practices under study? Such a process of reflection should include looping back to reexamine underlying assumptions behind problem definition (Argyris et al., 1985). Process validity must also deal with the much-debated problem of what counts as evidence to sustain assertions, as well as the quality of the relationships that are developed with participants.

Here, some criteria might be borrowed from naturalistic inquiry, depending on how evidence is defined. The notion of triangulation, or the inclusion of multiple perspectives, guards against viewing events in a simplistic or self-serving way. Triangulation also can refer to using a variety of methods—for example, observation and interviews—so that one is not limited to only one kind of data source. *Process* is not, however, limited to method. In narrative and essayist forms of inquiry, there are distinct criteria for what makes a good empirical narrative (as opposed to fiction). Connelly and Clandinin (1990) warn that "not only may one 'fake the data' and write a fiction but one may also use the data to tell a deception as easily as a truth" (p. 10). (See Connelly & Clandinin, 1990 for an elaboration of validity criteria for narrative research.)

Democratic validity refers to the extent to which research is done in collaboration with all parties who have a stake in the problem under investigation. If not done collaboratively, how are multiple perspectives and material interests taken into account in the study? For example, are teachers, nurses, social workers, or CEOs using action research to find solutions to problems that benefit them at the expense of other stakeholders? Are patients, clients, students, and community members seen as part of the insider community that undertakes this type of research, or are they viewed as outsiders by action researchers? Even when collaboration takes place, how deep does it go and how wide does it extend? While process validity depends on the inclusion of multiple voices for triangulation, democratic validity views it as an ethical and social justice issue.

Another version of democratic validity is what Cunningham (1983) calls "local" validity, in which the problems emerge from a particular context and in which solutions are appropriate to that context. Watkins (1991) calls this "relevancy" or "applicability" criteria for validity (i.e., How do we determine the relevance of findings to the needs of the problem context?) (p. 15). Drawing on Bronfenbrenner (1979), Tandon, Kelly, and Mock (2001) use the term "ecological validity," or the degree to which the constructs and products of the research are relevant to the participating group.

Catalytic validity is "the degree to which the research process reorients, focuses, and energizes participants toward knowing reality in order to transform it" (Lather, 1986b, p. 272). In the case of action research, not only the participants, but the researchers/practitioners themselves must be open to reorienting their view of reality as well as their view of their role. All involved in the research should deepen their understanding of the social reality under study and should be moved to some action to change it (or to reaffirm their support of it). The most powerful action research studies are those in which the researchers recount a spiraling change in their own and their participants' understandings. This reinforces the importance of keeping a research journal in which action researchers can monitor their own change process and consequent changes in the dynamics of the setting. While this criteria overlaps with process and democratic validity, it highlights the transformative potential of action research, which makes it so appealing to many critical pedagogues, organization and staff developers, and change agents.

Dialogic Validity. In academic research, the "goodness" of research is monitored through a form of peer review. Research reports must pass through the process of peer review in order to be disseminated through academic journals. Many academic journals even provide opportunities for researchers to engage in point-counterpoint debates about research. A similar form of peer review is beginning to develop within and among action research communities. Many action research groups are forming throughout North America, as action researchers seek dialogue with peers. In addition, publishing venues for action research have increased dramatically in the last decade.

In order to promote both democratic and dialogic validity, some have insisted that action research should only be done as collaborative inquiry (Torbert, 1981; Carr & Kemmis, 1986). Others simply suggest that action researchers participate in critical and reflective dialogue with other action researchers (Martin, 1987) or work with a critical friend who is familiar with the setting and can serve as devil's advocate for alternative explanations of research data. When the dialogic nature of practitioner inquiry is stressed, then studies can achieve what Myers (1985) calls "goodness-of-fit with the intuitions of the practitioner community, both in its definition of problems and in its findings" (p. 5).[5]

All of these validity criteria for action research are tentative and in flux. We agree with Connelly and Clandinin (1990), who, in discussing validity criteria for narrative inquiry, state,

> We think a variety of criteria, some appropriate to some circumstances and some to others, will eventually be the agreed-upon norm. It is currently the case that each inquirer must search for and defend the criteria that best apply to his or her work. (p. 7)

In the next section, we discuss how another set of authors, Reason and Bradbury (2001a), frame issues of validity and quality.

Reason and Bradbury's Discussion of Validity and Choice Points

Reason and Bradbury's (2001a) discussion of validity overlaps to some extent with the criteria we presented in the previous section, but there are important

Table 4.2   Broadening the Bandwidth of Validity

Dimensions of a Participatory Worldview	Characteristics of Action Research	Questions for Validity and Quality
Participatory evolutionary reality	Emergent developmental form	Questions of emergence and enduring consequence
Meaning and purpose	Human flourishing	Questions about significance
Extended epistemology	Knowledge-in-action	Questions about plural ways of knowing
Practical being and acting	Practical issues	Questions of outcome and practice
Relational ecological form	Participation and democracy	Questions of relational practice

Source: Bradbury and Reason, 2001a.

differences in emphasis. While ours were developed out of more insider action research studies, theirs were developed out of their experience with PAR and a view of action research as a worldview as well as a methodology. They identified five categories, based on what they call a "participatory worldview which we believe is emerging at this historical moment [and that] undercut[s] the foundations of the empirical-positivist worldview that has been the foundation of Western inquiry since the enlightenment (Toulman, 1990)" (p. 4).

While we can only give a cursory summary of their ambitious postpositivist project, we refer readers to Reason and Bradbury's Introduction and Conclusion of their important *Handbook of Action Research* (2001a). The *Handbook* provides exemplars of the multiple approaches to action research and their implications for creating indicators of quality. It also illustrates the extent to which action research is an international phenomenon.

Given that universities are concerned with knowledge generation, the dissertation will necessarily place this knowledge-oriented aspect of action research at its center. However, Reason and Bradbury (2001a) see action research as more than mere research and more than mere action. They see action research as an "emergent, evolutionary and educational process of engaging with self, persons and communities that needs to be sustained for a significant period of time" (p. 12). This leads to questions about validity and quality that center on emergence and enduring consequences of the research for self, persons, and communities. (See Table 4.2 for a summary of how these are linked.)

Reason and Bradbury (2001a) also promote a version of outcome validity that frames quality as questions of *outcome and practice*. Their focus on *relational practice* overlaps with what we have called *democratic validity,* which requires involving and honoring the perspectives of all parties who have a stake in the problem under investigation. They also see action research as producing not only conceptual knowledge, but also as exploring *new ways of knowing.* In this sense, validity claims are linked to "different forms of knowing in themselves and the relationship between different ways of knowing" (p. 12). Finally, they give the meaning and purpose of the research importance in terms of whether it has addressed *questions about significance.* As Greene (1992) points out, the real issue for action researchers is less "getting it right" than "making it meaningful" (p. 39).

Heron (1996), who has collaborated with Reason, takes an approach to validity similar to Bradbury and Reason, but with some unique characteristics. He approaches validity issues as a response to what he calls "uncritical subjectivity." He also rejects positivist notions of validity, but argues that all inquiry must address validity issues.

> The challenge after positivism is to redefine truth and validity in ways that honour the generative, creative role of the human mind in all forms of knowing. This also means, I believe, taking inquiry beyond justification, beyond the validation of truth-values, towards the celebration and bodying forth of being-values, as the transcendent and polar complement to the quest for validity. (p. 13)

Central to the validity of Heron's notion of *cooperative inquiry* is the notion of *research cycling* over time. Research cycling is similar to the ethnographer's notion of prolonged engagement with the field, but involves a more dialectical, dynamic engagement with participants. In cooperative inquiry,

> research outcomes are well-grounded if the focus of the inquiry, both in its parts and as a whole, is taken through as many cycles as possible by as many group members as possible, with as much individual diversity as possible and collective unity of approach as possible. (p. 131)

To even a greater extent than PAR, Heron's approach to cooperative inquiry, which is based on a cocounseling model, places a high value on the relational aspects of the research. For a study to have validity, authentic relationships must be maintained between group members and the initiating researchers as well as among group members themselves.

What is clear from these emerging approaches to criteria for the quality of action research is that they depart from current validity criteria for both quantitative and qualitative approaches to research. This is in part because of the unique concerns that action researchers have with workability, change, and empowerment and in part because they find the validity criteria of the social sciences is too limited. What is needed, however, is greater dialogue with research participants, including practitioners, in the construction of validity criteria.

Addressing Bias in Action Research

In a dissertation, it will be necessary to address how one's bias is dealt with in the research. This may be somewhat different for the student who is an insider to the setting than the student who is an outsider doing participatory research. Reason (1994) describes an approach to validity from humanistic psychology that he calls "critical subjectivity," which he distinguishes from both "the naïve subjectivity of 'primary process' awareness and the attempted objectivity of egoic 'secondary process' awareness" (p. 327). In other words, as researchers we acknowledge that we all enter research with a perspective drawn from our own unique experiences and so we articulate to the best of our ability these perspectives or biases and build a critical reflexivity into the research process. We also articulate these evolving perspectives in our journaling, field notes, and, to some extent, in the dissertation itself. Developing the skills and habits of self-reflexivity is necessary for any action researcher.

So while bias and subjectivity are natural and acceptable in action research as long as they are critically examined rather than ignored, other mechanisms may need to be put in place to ensure that they do not have a distorting effect on outcomes. Lomax, Woodward, and Parker (1996) establish the importance of validation meetings in which ongoing findings are defended before one or more critical friends, who serve as a kind of devil's advocate. Bone (1996), who did an action research study for his dissertation, describes a validation meeting:

> I asked three people to act as critical friends; one was my deputy, one was a member of staff, and the other was from outside the school, a friend who was also a business consultant. I selected my critical friends in order to get a range of different responses to my work. They helped me reflect on my practice and validate my research claims. (p. 156)

Grounded in Winter's (1989) narrative methodology and Whitehead's (1989) living theory approach, British practitioner researcher Evans's (1995) dissertation uses what she calls "memory work" to help her gain distance from her own taken-for-granted understandings of her practice. She forms her data into fictional stories which serve to provide both anonymity and sufficient distance to theorize her data. The stories help her identify patterns in her data and the stories are read back to the participants for validation. Not only was story used to contribute to the theorization of her data, but it was also used as a way to facilitate professional learning with her staff. She suggests that as practitioners begin to experience the contradictions between their values and their actions, their need to resolve these contradictions drives their research.

> I believe that my values lead my actions in moving towards a more fulfilling and satisfying way of life for me, and for those with whom I work. I am driven to change my practices because I recognize that they do not reflect fully my values, and I therefore feel ill at ease with myself. I take steps to change my actions and the way in which I see and think about my actions. . . . I believe that this is a value-laden, educational process—that I am taking part in an educational enquiry to get in touch with and live more fully my values about being a deputy head and supporting teaching and learning. It is educational because I act to change myself according to the values to which I am committed. (p. 270)

Evans is quick to add, however, that she cannot do this alone. "I need a group of people to challenge my thinking, to put alternative points of view, to point out inconsistencies in my thinking, to make problematic the assumptions I have taken for granted" (p. 270). To the extent that action researchers have positions high in the institutional hierarchy or are high-status outside change agents, such mechanisms become increasingly important. Where power differences are great, interviews become public performances in which subordinates tell the powerful what they want to hear (Scott, 1990). Action researchers use many of the techniques popular with qualitative researchers, such as triangulation of methods and data sources and member checking (Lincoln & Guba, 1985). However, because of the unique positionality of action researchers, further measures are sometimes necessary to establish the trustworthiness of the research.

Are the Findings of Action Research Generalizable?

There are many ways to approach the question of how results of action research are generalized, or transferred to other settings (often referred to as external validity), but we will suggest one taken from the work of Robert Stake (1986) on *naturalistic generalization*. Although Stake developed this approach to generalization in the context of qualitative, responsive, evaluation research, we feel it has powerful implications for action researchers. Stake's concept of naturalistic generalization is similar in many ways to Lincoln and Guba's (1985) notion of transferability, in which findings are not generalized, but rather transferred from a sending context to a receiving context. According to Lincoln and Guba,

> if there is to be transferability, the burden of proof lies less with the original investigator than with the person seeking to make an application elsewhere. The original inquirer cannot know the sites to which transferability might be sought, but

the appliers can and do. The best advice to give to anyone seeking to make a transfer is to accumulate *empirical* evidence about contextual similarity; the responsibility of the original investigator ends in providing sufficient descriptive data to make such similarity judgments possible. (p. 298)

Greenwood and Levin (1998) discuss this notion under the term *transcontextual credibility*. Although similar to the notion of transferability, Stake's elaboration of naturalistic generalization is more closely tied to *action* and therefore will serve our purposes here better. After years of well-documented failure by outside experts to bring about planned change in schools, Stake argues that it is time to rediscover the lessons about change that Dewey (1916, cited in Stake, 1986) taught us:

> Almost absent from mention in the "change literature" is the common way in which improvement is accomplished, a way followed intuitively by the greatest, and the least, of our thinkers. It is the experiential way, an evolutionary way, recognized particularly by John Dewey. One may change practice when *new experience* causes re-examination of problems: Intuitively we start thinking of alternative solutions. (Stake, 1986, p. 90)

Besides Dewey, Stake cites the work of Polanyi (1958) and Schon (1983), who argue that practice is guided less by formal knowledge than by personal knowledge based on personal or vicarious experience. They also argue that resistance to change is often a form of personal protection.

Stake's argument stipulates that action or changes in practice usually occur as a result of either some kind of external demand or coercion or the conviction on the part of practitioners that an action or change is necessary. We have seen time and again how coercion is successfully resisted by practitioners, and how most lasting change takes place through internal conviction or, to use a more popular term, ownership. A further premise is that a practitioner's internal conviction is influenced by a mixture of personal understanding and personal feeling or faith (voluntarism). Understanding, a primary goal of action research, is arrived at through dialogue and reflection drawing on two kinds of knowledge: experiential and propositional. These two kinds of knowledge, according to Stake (1986), are tied to two kinds of generalization: formalistic and naturalistic. "Continuing the analysis, we might say that theory and codified data are the main constituents of our formal, verbalized generalizations—whereas experience, real and vicarious, is the main constituent of the naturalistic generalizations" (p. 97).

To summarize this highly condensed chain of influence, *action* is influenced by *internal conviction,* which comes from *voluntarism* and *personal understanding.* This, in turn, is achieved by both *formalistic* and *naturalistic generalization,* the latter being the result of *direct* and *vicarious experience.* In

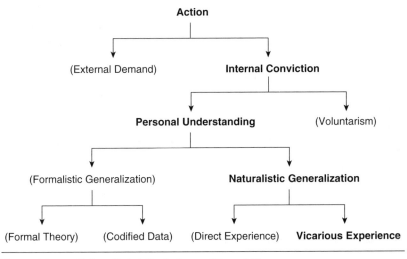

Figure 4.1   Robert Stake's Evolutionary View of Change

other words, practitioners tend to find traditional research, which is based on formalistic generalizations, less useful than narrative accounts from schools and classrooms that provide them with vicarious experience. Stake (1986) describes how naturalistic generalization is different from more traditional, formalistic generalization:

> The intention of most educational research is to provide formalistic generalization. A typical research report might highlight the correlation between time spent on team projects *and* gain in scores on an achievement test. The report might identify personality, affective and demographic variables. Even with little emphasis on causation this report is part of the grand explanation of student learning. It provides one way of knowing about educational practice.
>
> A more naturalistic research report might deal with the same topic, perhaps with the same teachers and pupils, yet reflecting a different epistemology. The naturalistic data would describe the actual interactions within student teams. The report would probably report project work—conveying style, context, and evolution. A person would be described as an individual, with uniqueness not just in deviance scores, but as a key to understanding the interactions. A reader senses the experience of teamwork in this particular situation. It is a *unique* situation in some respects, but ordinary in other respects. Readers recognize similarities with situations of their own. Perhaps they are stimulated to think of old problems in a new way. (pp. 98–99)

This type of research fits well with current practitioner culture where, although less systematic, stories are shared daily among practitioners as part of an oral craft tradition.

Likewise, Mishler (1986) suggests that the structure of the story is built into the human mind much like deep structures of grammar, and it is largely through narratives that humans make sense of and express their understanding of events and experiences.

We have limited our discussion to certain issues relating to what positivists call the internal and external validity of action research. There are many other issues, issues such as how action research generates, tests, or extends social theory, or to what extent action research studies can and should be replicated by other researchers. There are also other ways to think about and justify a study's external validity. We have provided Stake's approach because we find it a compelling way to think about how action research is taken up by other practitioners and researchers.

The Politics of Action Research

Although the politics of action research is only marginally related to its validity or trustworthiness, action researchers tend to have to deal with politics to a greater extent than those whose research approaches emphasize a more distanced stance vis-à-vis the research setting. Therefore, we have included this section here, because some will view the ways that action research is political to be a threat to its validity. We are not suggesting that any research is without politics, but because of its action-orientation and participatory nature, those who do action research have a special need to be aware of its effects.

When we talk about the politics of action research, we mean several things. First, action research is usually conducted in institutions nested in communities. All institutions are inherently political, and the micropolitics of institutions will inevitably be encountered by researchers. This institutional aspect of action research, we feel, has been generally glossed over in most of the literature.

Second, as practitioners begin to be involved in action research, either as researchers or participants, they begin to critique the narrowness of current definitions of their roles. The work of nurses, doctors, social workers, and teachers is becoming more fragmented, more supervised, more assessed, and consequently more controlled from the outside. The attempt to gain control over and redefine one's profession is an essentially political move.

Next, the question of who creates knowledge is a political question. Time and again we hear how inaccessible and irrelevant most of the knowledge created by nonparticipatory outside researchers is for practitioners and communities. Much of what practitioners know about their practice is "subjugated knowledge" (Foucault, 1980), or knowledge that is not viewed as valid by those who create knowledge in universities and by those who make policy. We live in a time when subjugated knowledge is being brought to light. Programs in women's studies and various ethnic studies programs are demanding legitimacy for diverse cultural and gendered ways of knowing. The knowledge of practitioners and their clients and communities is a form of subjugated knowledge because it is seldom given legitimacy by those who make policy.

And fourth, underlying all of these political aspects of action research is the ultimate need to problematize many of the purposes or functions of various social and professional practices and of our social institutions. Because action research is done in local settings, there is a need to understand the local in terms of macropolitical forces and social structural constraints. In the following sections, we discuss each of these issues in greater detail.

INSTITUTIONAL MICROPOLITICS

When practitioners say that their workplace is political, they are usually talking about what we are here calling micropolitics. Micropolitics includes the behind-the-scenes negotiations over material resources, vested interests, and ideological commitments. More often, micropolitical struggles are over such things as professional jealousy, power differences in the organizational hierarchy, the allocation of space and other resources, gender and racial politics, and so forth. Micropolitics is what gets talked about in private among practitioners; it is also what never gets talked about at meetings because it is too "political." Micropolitics often exist within the silences that are created in institutions. It is as much about what doesn't get said as it is about what does. Those who do organizational action research tend to build these issues into their research and are trained to deal with them. However, given its potential for asking critical questions, moving beyond the initial questions and study site, and challenging power relations, action research should not be undertaken ingenuously.

Unanticipated side effects occur even when the research has been carefully contained. For instance, one middle school teacher found that when she began interviewing her students and engaging them in a collaborative study of their own classroom, the students started asking similar questions of teachers in other classrooms. This caught other teachers off guard and they correctly attributed it to the teacher's research project. Action research, like all good qualitative research, has a natural tendency to spill over into areas one had not expected to study. Action research is by nature holistic, and, therefore, it cannot easily be used to study a phenomenon independent of the various layers of social context within which it is situated.

The institutional politics of action research rub up against what Schon (1971, cited in Holly, 1989) calls the "dynamic conservatism" of social institutions. According to Schon,

> A social system is a complex of individuals which tends to maintain its boundaries and its patterns of internal relationships. But given internal tendencies towards increasing disorder, and external threats to stability, energy must be expended if the patterns of the system are to be held stable. Social systems are self reinforcing systems which strive to remain in something like equilibrium. . . . Social systems resist change with an energy roughly proportional to the radicalness of the change that is threatened. (p. 80)

Action researchers working individually or collaboratively are often ill prepared for the resistance (sometimes in the form of indifference) to their efforts. They encounter an institutional culture that values individual effort, professional isolation, and conformity.

THE POLITICS OF REDEFINING PROFESSIONALISM

This section refers primarily to action research in which practitioners study their own settings, either alone, collaboratively with other professionals, or with outside change agents. Action or practitioner research has been put forward as a way to reprofessionalize practice in the face of increasing attempts to standardize and deskill professional work (Cochran-Smith & Lytle, 1993). In this section, we will briefly explore what it has meant historically for practitioners to gain professional status and what it might mean today for practitioners to rethink what it means to be a professional.

The move by many professions to adopt a university model led to shifts in how professional knowledge was produced and valued. We will take an example from education, where normal schools and teachers colleges were abandoned in favor of university status. As this process occurred, colleges of education increasingly adopted the arts and sciences' definitions of valid knowledge over that of educational practitioners. Gitlin et al. (1992) state,

> Challenges to the normal school were based on both their practice emphasis and the inclusion of women in those institutions. To achieve professional status required not only a move away from practice toward scientific research, but also a move to differentiate the work of teachers, commonly seen as women's work, from the educational leadership positions held mostly by men. (p. 80)

According to Schon (1983), there is a crisis of confidence in most professions.

> When leading professionals write or speak about their own crisis of confidence, they tend to focus on the mismatch of traditional patterns of practice and knowledge to features of the practice situation—complexity, uncertainty, instability, uniqueness, and value conflict—of whose importance they are becoming increasingly aware. (p. 18)

This crisis of confidence comes, in part, from trying to force a definition of professionalism that values problem solving over problem framing, scientific knowledge over personal knowledge, and facts over values onto a professional reality which is messy, intuitive, anecdotal, and value laden. As reflective models of practice replace the old social engineer and craft models of practice, an action research model of professionalism gains validity.

THE POLITICS OF KNOWLEDGE

Closely related to the empowerment of practitioners and communities is the issue of who creates knowledge, how it is created, and who uses it for what purposes. These are all political questions. In postmodern terms, the knowledge of communities and practitioners is subjugated knowledge, along with the knowledge of other marginalized groups such as women, the poor, and some ethnic and racial groups.

Planners think in terms of knowledge created in universities or research and development centers, which is then disseminated or diffused into organizations, where it is implemented or utilized by practitioners. Planners hope this process will result in the institutionalization of their research-backed innovations. Reformers are now realizing that including practitioners in these efforts through collaborative action research projects is a more appropriate way to proceed, but many practitioners fear that this is just a more sophisticated implementation strategy. Rather than be empowered by outsiders, many practitioners are arguing that they must assert their own claims to the creation of legitimate knowledge. Rather than be invited to participate in projects initiated in universities and research and development centers, they want to initiate the projects and, as needed, invite those outsiders with specialized knowledge to participate. However, as practitioners move to reassert their professional prerogatives, they must be sensitive to others, such as clients, patients, employees, or communities, who are also "experts" about their own experiences and needs.

THE MACROPOLITICS OF ACTION RESEARCH PROJECTS

Action research projects are usually initiated because of some practical problem in a local setting. However, local problems and local settings are parts of larger problems and broader social forces that not only impact local settings but are implicated in how local settings are constituted. An example of how local settings are impacted is the research on social capital.

Stanton-Salazar (2001) and others have found that the social mobility of individuals depends in part on their social networks and the social capital these networks provide. More economically privileged individuals enjoy strong social networks through their extended families, friendship groups, and workplace relations. Low-income individuals depend more on institutional agents, such as teachers, counselors, social workers, public heath workers, librarians, and community leaders for the kind of social capital that leads to upward social mobility. Low-income individuals do have social networks and accrue social capital (and cultural capital), but their social and cultural capital does not provide them with entrée into privileged settings. Their cultural and social capital has a low exchange value among those institutional agents who act as gatekeepers to upward social mobility. So, for instance, if a high school counselor does not inform certain students about college opportunities, those students' lack of social capital may make college appear to be an unattainable goal.

The solution may appear to be obvious. Train counselors to better understand their gatekeeper role so they can distribute social capital more equitably to students. However, in an age in which the welfare state is being rolled back and social programs are being cut, there will continue to be fewer institutional agents available for low-income individuals. In low-income neighborhoods, the lack of public libraries, community centers, affordable preschool programs, and sufficient funding for schools means that institutional agents that were more available to a previous generation are no longer available, particularly in urban communities of color. So is the problem one of retraining institutional agents or addressing changes at the level of state and national policy or both? It may be that to address one without addressing the other will not solve the problem. At a structural level, one needs to understand the ideological shifts that replaced the postwar Keynesian social contract between labor and industry with a neoliberal, free market, postwelfarist ideology in the mid 1970s.

Including an analysis of such macro-level forces in action research projects may bring accusations of overtheorizing data or promoting an ideological agenda. However, to ignore such forces is also to politicize one's research through blaming the victim by individualizing or psychologizing a problem whose causes are ultimately social and/or economic. In order to understand the local, one must understand how the local came to be the way it is. This will necessarily take the action researcher into an analysis that is social, historical, and economic. It will also provide a more complex understanding of where solutions are to be sought.

As we have illustrated in this section, politics comes in many forms and exists on many levels. Humans inhabit a political world in much the same way that fish inhabit water. Sometimes it is so obvious we don't see it, or we have been taught not to see it. It is in this sense that all research is political. To ignore politics is to place one's project and the validity of one's analysis at risk. We realize that politics is a minefield and that, by now, action research may seem like a daunting task. In the following chapter, we will provide the closest we will come in this book to offering a nuts-and-bolts account of how action research dissertations are designed, carried out, and defended.

5

Designing the
Plane While Flying it

Proposing and Doing the Dissertation

There is a sense in which all good social research has certain things in common. Good research deals with significant issues and attempts to answer significant questions about the issues. It participates in a larger conversation about the issue, resulting in a review of previous research and theory that informs the research question. It demonstrates a sound methodological approach with appropriate forms of validity. It provides some kind of evidence for inferences, draws implications, and makes recommendations for future study and practice.

But as others (Maguire, 1993; Reason & Marshall, 2001) have suggested, action research can also move beyond the standard stated above and will, ideally, intersect with one's own growth areas and values and beliefs. While it is not uncommon for academics to leave themselves off the page in terms of the personal origins and impact of the research, Reason and Marshall (2001) suggest otherwise when discussing action research:

> All good research is *for me, for us,* and *for them:* it speaks to three audiences. . . . It is *for them* to the extent that it produces some kind of generalizable ideas and outcomes which elicit the response "That's interesting!" from those who are concerned to understand a similar field (Davis, 1971). It is *for us* to the extent that it responds to concerns for our praxis, is relevant and timely, and so produces the response, "That works!" from those who are struggling with problems in their field of action. It is *for me* to the extent that the process and outcomes respond directly to the individual researcher's being-in-the-world, and so elicit the response, "That's exciting"—taking exciting back to its root meaning, to set in action. (Reason & Marshall, 1987, pp. 112–113, original emphasis, cited in Reason & Marshall, 2001)

If they choose to engage in action research, then, researchers can expect that their work will contribute to their sense of being-in-the world, to their praxis, and to the larger conversation regarding the topic under study as well as the process of inquiry.

The Dissertation Proposal

The proposal and the dissertation are, initially, aimed at an audience of a few people: the doctoral student's dissertation committee. As we have discussed in earlier chapters, there may be a greater need to justify an action research approach in the proposal because committee members and dissertation chairs are less likely to be familiar with it than with traditional methodologies that have greater credibility within social science disciplines. Action research has, at times, been relegated to a lesser status—something that can inform practice but not an approach that contributes to a larger knowledge base, which is one of the explicit goals of dissertation research (Anderson & Herr, 1999).

While it may be ideal to have as a mentor a dissertation chair who is steeped in action research, or even one who initiates a large action research project that students can be a part of, as was the case for Lynne Mock (see chapter 6), that may not be within the realm of possibilities for many students. Maguire (1993) suggests that doctoral students seek out faculty who are at least open to action research if not fully conversant with it. The goal in this case would be to work together in threading a way through the action research dissertation process rather than obstructing or distorting it.

A dissertation is written with a particular audience in mind and in a field of study that implies certain conventions of writing and research. While joining a larger discipline of study—social work, psychology, education, and so forth—a doctoral student's research is taking place in a local context, grounded in a sense of what is possible in one's own college and university. A doctoral student is well served by "reading" the local context for dissertation studies by exploring what others who have come before were able to do and with whom, while also acknowledging the research conventions within the larger context of specific academic disciplines.

Typically, an action research proposal will more closely resemble one by a qualitative than a quantitative researcher, because, as with qualitative research, the design is emergent. While quantitative dissertation proposals must have the first three chapters written in final form, both qualitative and action research proposals must begin the research with a clear direction but with the anticipation that as data gathering and analysis proceed, the questions, methods, design, and participants may all shift somewhat. In fact, for action research, these shifts are anticipated as part of the spiraling synergism of action and understanding. As these cycles of research spiral over time, new questions, new literature, and new methods emerge. How to bound this process into a dissertation is ultimately the task of the doctoral student, but it cannot be easily predicted at the proposal stage.

A good action research dissertation proposal will provide sufficient literature to frame the initial problem and anticipate directions the research might take. In action research, the problems themselves tend to drive the research to an equal or greater extent than the literature. For this reason, action research, like much grounded-theory research, is often seen as more data-driven than theory-driven. Again, seeking balance while accommodating the expectations of the dissertation committee and institutional review board (IRB) is the goal. While entering the study in a too open-ended fashion is an invitation to chaos, letting the literature provide too narrow a focus is also a problem. Overreliance on the lens that the literature provides on the problem under study can keep the researcher from seeing things that do not conform to expectations that the literature set up.

Ideally, graduate students should begin to "pilot" an action research study while still taking coursework. We place *pilot* in quotes because, unlike traditional research, it is often hard to distinguish a pilot study from the real thing. In action research, a pilot study is likely to simply be early cycles of research in an ongoing research spiral. It may be useful, however, to use the language of pilot studies in a dissertation proposal. Because action research is labor intensive and because it takes time to build the relationships and structures needed, it is difficult to start from scratch at the dissertation proposal stage. For those doing action research in their own sites, the problem is less severe, but it is even more likely that such easy access to one's site would ensure laying groundwork for the research prior to completing doctoral coursework. One thing is certain: Action research seldom fits neatly into the one mythical dissertation year that follows coursework. Doing a series of pilot studies in preparation for the dissertation year can increase the chances of finishing in a timely manner.

This piloting lets the doctoral student try on research questions and methodologies; the initial data gathering and analysis can help guide the ongoing direction of the overall research. This pilot material can all be seen as part of the action research process, and the results of these pilots can be part of both the proposal and the dissertation. In essence, a doctoral student is saying, "I did this and this is where it has taken me thus far. This is what I learned." The proposed research for the dissertation can be an outgrowth of this earlier work, nested in what became clearer through the piloting. This can include a trying on of methodological approaches, the data analysis, how to deal with one's own positionality, and so forth. But the dissertation research must add a new piece to what the student has already done and come to know. In other words, we want to make clear that the pilot studies do not add up to the actual dissertation, but rather set the stage for it.

Where Do Action Research Questions Come From?

As we mentioned earlier, action research questions reflect our interests and concerns on multiple levels—Reason and Marshall's (2001) idea that the research is *for them, for us, for me.* Action researchers, then, should expect that their research questions will cut across and introduce the possibilities for change on multiple levels. For the action researcher, this can be an intimate undertaking, consistent and congruent with ways we see ourselves in the world and the things that are important to us. For example, in stating her belief that the research we do cannot be disconnected from our values and philosophy, Maguire (1993) writes of her own dissertation research, "I started out looking for ways to make my dissertation research more congruent with my beliefs about empowerment and social justice" (176). She chose to do participatory action research (PAR) as a way of integrating her interests, values, and beliefs. Whereas some research approaches have suggested that researchers keep their passions and themselves out of the process, we are suggesting that the questions we pursue in action research are often related to our own quandaries and passions.

> The motivation to research may arise from existential commitments in students' lives; they are committed to work with issues of race or gender, to manage in ways that are collaborative and inquiring, to address the crisis of ecological sustainability. Often they know intuitively or tacitly what it is they want to research, but their definition of the project is typically too loose, too formal, too presented for outside consumption to really take off. The project needs to touch their heart in some way if it is to sustain them. (Reason & Marshall, 2001, p. 415)

We would infer from this that action research questions often start with the students and/or have big implications for them as beings-in-the-world. They can expect, then, in the process, an interrogation of themselves that results in change. In some of the following sections, we will address how issues play out differently for those students who are insiders—usually practitioners—to the setting under study than for those who are outsiders working in collaboration with insiders.

INSIDER ACTION RESEARCH

There is often a sense, in insider action research, that there is not a clear beginning or, for that matter, ending of the research. Research questions are often formalized versions of puzzles that practitioners have been struggling with for some time and perhaps even acting on in terms of problem solving. The decision to do more systematic inquiry on a puzzling issue is one of asking what issue or problem am I really trying to solve? How might data shed light on this? It is, in essence, a stepping back a bit from what is often a daily struggle or puzzle to gain perspective through systematic inquiry. Formalizing the puzzles of practice into research is a way of working better rather than doing more of the same only harder. What we are suggesting, then, is that many action research questions come out of a frustration, a practice puzzle, or a contradiction in a workplace (this is what we say we do, but do we?); often these are things a practitioner has been giving thought to for some time. The research question most often addresses something the practitioner wants to do better or understand more clearly. Battaglia (1995) believes that for practitioners who do action research, the questions themselves become part of a general attitude of inquiry.

> I now believe that Action Research is as much a process of asking questions about one's practice as it is deciding what to do about solutions. Action Research enables you to live your questions; in a way, they become the focal point of your thinking. My questions took on an almost mantra-like quality; they seemed to seep into my thinking and conversation, creep into my reading and writing when I'd least expect. They also kept me focused. I appreciate how professionally healthy it might be to adopt an "Action Research mentality" whereby one is always thinking about or attempting to polish another facet of the work one does. Perhaps, then, Action Research is an attitude or becomes an attitude that is brought to one's practice. (p. 89)

A research question can also be generated by an outside assessment of how well or poorly an agency, school, or bureaucracy is performing. Assessments of this kind often reflect standards that originate outside of the work site itself, with schools or agencies or bureaucracies being held accountable to a standard perhaps imposed via state or federal mandates or a funding source. In cases such as these, the action research question can reflect a more collective puzzle. Examples of this would include the faculty of a school being curious as to how they might raise student achievement levels or a juvenile detention facility wanting to reduce its rate of recidivism. Or, sometimes an intervention has already been put into place, based on workers' professional opinions and problem solving or via an assessing outside entity, and the agency is now wondering whether the intervention is working or how it might be refined. All of these are examples in which more than one person "owns" the question. It reflects collective curiosity regarding a part of the organization's functioning. One person, perhaps the doctoral student, may take the lead in instigating the inquiry, or it may be set in motion through a small team of interested people or stakeholders. An established committee or work unit already in place may be charged with coordinating the research effort. An alternate route could be an invitation to an outsider with research expertise to collaborate on the inquiry effort.

While action research is often best done collaboratively, dissertations are typically individual undertakings. A doctoral student may have an individual question within a larger, collective inquiry or produce the written account of the collective action research effort, taking responsibility for a systematic accounting and questioning of the research process. Because a doctoral student is invested in both the actions implemented to solve a workplace issue as well as in producing an artifact to satisfy dissertation requirements, it is not uncommon for a doctoral student to take responsibility for producing a document that goes beyond that of workplace knowledge. The dissertation that comes out of this kind of collective inquiry is a more public document, prepared for dissemination beyond the site. Issues to be considered in such an undertaking are the following: Who owns the data? Are all the stakeholders comfortable with the public dissemination of the data? Does the doctoral student need his or her own, individual research piece within the larger, collective study? In terms of this last question, it is a common arrangement for a doctoral student to create an individual piece or study within the larger inquiry; in this kind of situation, the doctoral student typically has access to the larger data set, collectively gathered, while also pursuing an individual version of the research question.

As with much of action research, we see this issue of who owns the data as an ongoing conversation and negotiation as the research evolves. At the same time, we would encourage doctoral students to initially work out agreements with other stakeholders regarding the use of data and its dissemination for the dissertation. To work toward clear agreements initially and then to continue to revisit the working understanding serves as a protection for the doctoral student and other stakeholders against any later confusion regarding intellectual property rights. Putting in writing these early agreements makes them explicit. The writing up of these agreements also teases out areas that might not have initially been considered or those that are not as clear as one thought. Again, action research is a complex process and the threading through of intellectual property rights is no exception. The goal is to have as upfront, clear working agreements and relationships as possible, early on in the process.

Even if a doctoral student starts with what seems to be an individual puzzle or concern, the posing of a research question in an institutional context or workplace typically spills beyond the individual. Others may become interested in the issue or feel threatened by the study (Herr, 1999b). When taking into account the context for the research question, it is not really possible to anticipate the direction the inquiry will take or the kinds of interests it will threaten or attract. Still, it is a good idea for individual insider researchers to consider the politics of their own context and who—including themselves—they may be putting at risk through their inquiry. Action research takes place in local contexts at given points in sociohistorical time, and the researcher will want to assess the risks in asking particular questions. This is important to consider because, once the action research is set in motion, the researcher should not assume its spiraling is under the researcher's control. One unique aspect of doing insider action research is that we are initiating research in a setting where we already have relationships; it may also be a place where we intend to stay for a long period of time, even if the research ends. Given these realities, insider researchers may ask themselves what research questions they want to take on and what feels too politically volatile to tackle at a given point in time.

We are suggesting that these realities factor into the decision to pursue one research question over another as the researcher juggles possible trade-offs and complexities. Depending on the context, the researcher may make the choice to pursue one question over another or deliberately put a question on a back burner to be considered at another time. Or, conversely, an issue may strike at the core of a researcher's ethics, or "bottom line," and, from that vantage point, beg to be interrogated through inquiry; in such cases, the researcher may decide to pursue a question because it is ethically difficult not to, even if it seems risky for the researcher professionally or personally.

OUTSIDER ACTION RESEARCH

This same sense of ethics or values may drive outside researchers to pursue action research because they want to not only generate knowledge, but also make a contribution to the setting they study. This activist stance may come out of a critique of the status quo and a desire to interrupt it; or a student may be driven by a theoretical stance, such as feminism or critical theory, that lends itself to an activist research stance. Students may first come to embracing action research as a way to avoid exploiting a population for research purposes (research *on* rather than *with*), and then decide on dissertation topics that lend themselves to that approach.

Students may want to piggyback on things they are already doing, places they have access to, or larger projects offered to them through faculty grants or through their own professional expertise. At the same time, convenient opportunities may seem like a pragmatic solution to producing a dissertation but may compromise one's passions or professional direction. Many graduate students have opportunities to participate in faculty research and grants and these can often serve as a vehicle for dissertation research; the question for doctoral students is whether these opportunities match their own professional goals for the dissertation.

It is not uncommon for students to initiate an intervention themselves and study it for the purposes of doing research as well as improving or impacting a setting. Saavedra (1996), for example, invited teachers into a study group for her dissertation research; the goal of the study group was

> to investigate how we could reconstruct classroom and school contexts by developing a more critical understanding of teaching and learning, and by recreating

our roles as educators to deal with the influences that social and institutional policies and practices have on our students. We sought to achieve this by cultivating a forum for ongoing collaboration and collective reflection, and by using a process of problem posing and problem solving of issues that affect student learning and empowerment. (p. 271)

Saavedra based her work on the premise that if teachers had opportunities for emancipatory learning and their own transformation as teachers, this experience could radically impact the way they approached the classrooms they then created.

Issues of Design and Methodology

In naturalistic inquiry, there is a sense that the methodology may evolve as it is implemented in the field, depending on the conditions that greet the researcher as the study is being implemented. With action research and the assumption of the research spiral, this premise of an evolving methodology is a virtual given. While the steps of the action research spiral may remain the same—that is, iterative cycles of plan-act-observe-reflect (Lewin, 1948)—these are broad categories or steps that will be translated into actions in the field. For example, as a researcher gains insight into the puzzle being studied, the next step may be to broaden the scope of the data gathering, something not previously anticipated by the researcher; this could be a step that now makes sense, derived from the researcher's reflection and understanding from the previous round of data gathering, analysis, and actions taken.

A dissertation committee must then give a student a degree of latitude in terms of the evolution of the methodology and where successive cycles of plan-act-observe-reflect take the research. The methodology section of the dissertation proposal is the researcher's best guess as to what will transpire in the field. In the dissertation, the doctoral student is then writing up the actual evolution of the research, documenting the decisions made. It is not uncommon, given these realities, that doctoral students will significantly rewrite what was originally written in the methodology section of the proposal for the dissertation. For the dissertation, students are writing a close account of what they actually did and the reasoning behind the methodological decisions they made.

Earlier we warned against a flawed approach to action research, what we called the outsider within, where the fact that the doctoral student is both a researcher and an actor/participant in the research is ignored; doctoral students in these cases are, in essence, asked to take themselves out of the research and pretend that they are not part of the action or activity. Because it is our strong belief that this leads to a problematic and inappropriate framing of the research, we suggest that as the doctoral student is laying out the proposal, a key piece of this work is to think through the doctoral student's multiple roles in the project—as researcher, as insider, perhaps as employee or facilitator, and so forth.

We suggest that this complexity of roles be brought into the research from the beginning and acknowledged rather than being rendered invisible. In the methodology section of the proposal, this complexity of roles is often addressed in a section regarding the researcher's positionality; by this we mean, Who is the researcher to the research process? What is the researcher bringing in terms of roles, values, beliefs, and experiences? Is the researcher an insider to the research? An outsider? Somewhere on the continuum? Who is the researcher in terms of hierarchy and status? How do these multiple positions impact the research design and process? We suggest spending time making sense of these questions as they apply to the proposed research and see this interrogation and documentation of self as the beginning of an ongoing task to be carried out throughout the research process.

Action research is characterized by its use of autobiographical data. If, for example, the research question is about their own professional practice or personal experience, researchers are clearly required to study themselves (Tenni, Smith & Boucher, 2003) or, if a researcher is the facilitator or instigator of a change process, part of the research documentation is the researcher's roles, actions, and decisions. Because of this lived complex reality, keeping a research journal is a vital piece of any action research methodology; it is a chronicle of research decisions; a record of one's own thoughts, feelings, and impressions; as well as a document reflecting the increased understanding that comes with the action research process. Beyond these, it is important to keep track of the ethical decisions made throughout the research process. As Reason and Bradbury (2001) suggest, "the primary 'rule' in Action Research practice is to be aware of the choices one is making and their consequences" (p. xxvii); this "rule," we would suggest, can at least in part be served by the keeping of a research journal that systematically records choices and their consequences for one's self and others.

Chairs and committee members must be comfortable acknowledging the student's multiple roles and suggesting appropriate epistemological and methodological approaches for the study, given this reality. Whereas, for example, action research may share with qualitative research some of the same data gathering techniques (interviews, content analysis of documents, etc.), this is not to be confused with being able to lift wholesale all the conventions of one research approach into another (consider, for example, validity criteria, as discussed in chapter 4.) Reason and Marshall (2001) suggest that in guiding the action research dissertation, faculty are asked to meet the student on multiple levels, not the least of which is the personal; professors are asked to help hold and honor the issues that emerge out of a student's *critical subjectivity* with the idea that this material can be drawn into the creative process of the research. Action research is a messy, somewhat unpredictable process, and a key part of the inquiry is a recording of decisions made in the face of this messiness. Because of this, doctoral students often feel vulnerable about capturing all of this in detail for their dissertation committee members to read and—so they fear—judge. In the face of this vulnerability, students will need reassurance from their committee members that the "perfect" dissertation research is the one where a good faith effort and commitment to the learning process is paramount as the intricacies of action research are attempted for perhaps the first time by the researcher. Because students may also need or request active guidance as they make their way in an unfolding process, dissertation chairs should anticipate that supervising an action research dissertation is likely to be more intense and relational than it is for more traditional dissertations.

Because action researchers are so involved in the research process at multiple levels and in multiple roles, it is common for action researchers to utilize critical friends (Anderson, Herr & Nihlen, 1994), or a validation team, and write this into the research process. These are usually peers or colleagues, rather than dissertation committee members, willing to debrief with the researcher, collaboratively make meaning, as well as pose questions regarding how it is that a researcher "knows" what it is he or she knows. Critical friends often push researchers to another level of understanding because they ask researchers to make explicit what they may understand on a more tacit level. Action researchers, because of the intensity and longevity of the research process, can use critical friends as vital sounding boards, to help them step back or out of the research enough to more thoroughly understand what it is they are seeing and doing.

DESIGNING INSIDER ACTION RESEARCH

Even if the proposed research has the endorsement of the institution for which one works or is affiliated with, it is the rare situation in which the primary job of a doctoral student is to be an action researcher. In other words, most insider action researchers are doing the inquiry while continuing to carry the rest of their workloads. Few of us get released or paid to additionally pursue our research, even if it benefits the institutions for which we work. Because of this lived reality, the methodological approach to the data gathering needs to be *researcher friendly*; by this we mean realistically doable, given the contexts and demands of our jobs.

In designing the action research project, one way to begin is to ask what is already known about the question or puzzle that is the focus of the inquiry. Institutions accumulate quite a paper trail, documenting through memos, statistical data, policy guides, external regulations, and the like—all of which can be analyzed in relationship to many of our research questions. Organizational mission statements are public documents and can also be utilized in comparing actual practices with an institution's stated aims. An action researcher will want to first explore what data have already been generated that have relevance to the proposed inquiry. In addition, it is good to take a look at what limits, or bounds, possible interventions and inquiry. For example, decisions may have been made at other levels (for example, World Bank, federal, or state) that put in place parameters or interventions that must be utilized to some degree. At the same time, there is often some latitude in these, and part of the task of the action researcher is to assess the "givens" and the "wiggle room." All of this information helps frame the inquiry and provides the broad outline within which the action research takes place.

Not all the data that a researcher uses have to be newly generated when the inquiry is formally initiated. Remember, we stated earlier that insider action research often feels like it has no clear beginning, meaning it often has been embedded in the problem solving of a practitioner or institution for some time; now that the problem solving is being moved to the level of explicit research, the researcher will want to nest the methodological approach within data that have already been gathered or are available. So the first question for the insider action researcher is this: What data are already available that have relevance for my study? The researcher can draw on both local knowledge, generated explicitly within the site of the study, as well as bigger data sets that document trends that might have relevance for the study getting under way. This is data for the researcher to access but not necessarily to generate.

A second question to ask is, What data are possible through the daily routines of work, things that the researcher does as part of the job? Since the research role is most often one that is in addition to the other things we do on the job, insider action researchers will want to take a hard look at the tasks they do, the routines they carry out, that can become part of data gathering if formally brought to that level of systematization. For example, record keeping in its various forms is always good to explore for its data generating properties. Because time for research is always somewhat limited, the researcher will want to see where it is possible to piggyback on what the job requires and what can be simultaneously used as part of the data set. The following is Jackie Delong's (2002) description of her database, gathered over a 6-year period largely as part of her job. Delong was a superintendent of a school district in Canada when she wrote her dissertation under the supervision of Jack Whitehead at Bath University in England. Her dissertation, along with several others, is available on Whitehead's website.

The research database, which includes some quantitative but, primarily, qualitative data, is extensive. It includes journals expressed as e-mails, case studies, audio and videotapes, transcripts of meetings and interviews, meeting minutes, surveys, reports and policy and procedure documents, print, video and electronic publications—mine and other's, film and digital photographs, and validation responses and meetings. Over the six years, I have kept journals, daily and often more than once a day, of my activities and reflections by means of e-mails to Jack Whitehead. This was part of the dialogical process. I also have records of e-mails to other academics and professionals that serve to show the progress of various directions in my work and life. I have found that I need an audience for my thoughts as well as a respondent.

Over several months late in 2000, I read and reviewed and sifted and reflected on my collection of data spread over an old pool table extended via other surfaces. Visiting and revisiting the data has been essential to understanding because it is "difficult for the Action Researcher to grasp everything at once and data may need to be revisited in the light of new experiences" (James, 1999). I re-read and reflected on my narratives of school board amalgamation, supporting Action Research projects, creating the masters program in partnership with Brock University, my published writings and validation papers, my performance evaluations and looked with new eyes at the hundreds of photos I'd taken over the six years. (Delong, 2002, p. 283)

Having answered the questions—What data already exist and what data do daily work routines generate?—the researcher can then begin to ask what data gathering needs to be explicitly added or generated for this particular research. This is the place where the researcher is choosing what can be realistically added to a workday in the name of the action research. While we are encouraging action researchers to be somewhat pragmatic in their data-gathering approaches, and are cognizant of the time constraints full-time employees face, at the same time we firmly believe that good action research is also a relief in that the data generated—and the analysis—can help in working *better*. Action research, then, can be a trade-off of sorts, trading in daily practices that are not yielding as positive a result as hoped in the name of improved practices generated by the data.

Data analysis begins immediately and guides further data gathering and decision making. One tension for the insider researcher is that decisions for action must sometimes be made before the researcher has reached a thorough understanding of the data; this is particularly true if the research question is a collaborative one or one where decisions will be made by a designated group in the setting. In such cases, the researcher must choose whether to speak out based on what is already known through the research, albeit an unfinished analysis, or miss the opportunity entirely to influence the direction of unfolding practices and decisions. The realities and timelines of the practice setting often collide with the researcher's desire for more time for reflection and meaning making. To be able to freeze-frame the whole endeavor while further analysis is pursued is not often a luxury offered to the action researcher; in part, one's task is to speak out of what one has discovered thus far while holding the awareness that the data and analysis have more to offer than what one has currently had the chance to thoroughly explore. There are multiple layers to the data analysis process: the initial meaning making, including some decisions regarding directions for interventions or actions; and then a revisiting of the data for a more thorough, holistic understanding. The latter analysis takes the researcher beyond the initial level of understanding. The following quote from Delong's (2002) methodology chapter illustrates this holistic approach to data.

In my work, whether it be delegating a task to someone or committing to the process of accomplishing a task through a committee or project management team, I have to trust the process. I have frequently advised groups who are undertaking practitioner research to just let the action-reflection process, the journaling and dialogue with critical friends, and the writing and sharing happen, to trust the process. Amazing how difficult it is to take your own advice. I now know that I can trust the process. The actual writing, reflecting, dialoguing, revising, and revising again, has created my knowing. At the beginning of writing, I had masses of research data, a messy rummage of thoughts and ideas, confusion and chaos, and an excruciating need for order and clarity.

You would laugh if you could see the family/recreation room that I converted to a writing centre for the writing of this thesis. . . . There is no order or clarity here. The reason it works for me is that I am a holistic thinker and need the picture of the whole before I can deal with the pieces. It is one of the reasons I struggled with the learning of math in high school from very sequential teachers. I was thirty-five years old and an occasional teacher teaching classes of business math when I realized this. So having chart paper on the walls with timelines and themes and all my research data, books, publications and photos spread out visibly was an essential environment for me to write.

I wrote the thesis the same way that I live and work—with intensity. With the exception of short breaks such as walks, conversations with my friends and children, I usually wrote for eight to ten hours a day, weekends and holidays. I found an hour here and there was not productive. Because of the random nature of my thinking processes (Delong & Wideman, 1996), I usually worked on three or four documents on the computer screen at once plus the references page and the parking lot, and pulled a new one up as I found a connection to another. I would move back and forth between my data, the literature, thinking, writing, and revising.

I did not separate the literature search into a separate compartment as in the traditional academic search but engaged with the academic research as it came into the subject of the writing or triggered some critical judgments in my data analysis, synthesis and evaluation. . . . My train of thought being what it is, more like a moving target than a straight line, I kept a section at the end of each document called "Parking Lot." As a new idea, memory, image, or connection would wash though my mind, I would "park" it in the parking lot and come back to it later. This process was similar to what Ron Wideman and I came up with as we worked on the book *Action Research: School Improvement Through Research-Based Professionalism* (1998b), only in that case to retain my random thoughts and to keep us on task I used post-it notes stuck on the table. This process of parking an idea or process is reflected in my life. When a project is not working, I park it until the constellation of factors that will make it come together emerge. (pp. 287–289)

DESIGNING OUTSIDER ACTION RESEARCH

Being an outsider in the action research process can still imply a wide range in terms of the researcher's positionality and stance toward the research. Much depends on whether relationships are already established or the researcher is working to newly access possible participants, and the kinds of relationships the researcher seeks to establish. In chapter 3, drawing on the work of Cornwall (1996), we outlined a range of possible relationships between the outside researcher and the potential participants in the research. These relationships vary along a continuum in terms of who sets the agenda for the research and who are in decision-making roles. For researchers to locate themselves, we pose questions such as, Whose research question is it and where did it come from? How did the researcher come to be involved? Did the researcher initiate the research or was he or she invited to participate by a local group? What kind of relationships does the researcher want to cultivate with others involved in the process? What are the goals of the research in terms of actions derived from it or as part of the process?

The answers to the questions posed above have repercussions in terms of the direction of the research methodology. If, for example, a researcher conceives of the research question and then designs an intervention with a group, the research question may not be organic to the group itself; in this case, the group cooperates with the researcher, contributing data, while also being involved in a process that could have repercussions for them. The researcher remains very much in charge of the research and change process and is working to cultivate goodwill with the group in the hope of their participation; at the same time, the researcher has something to offer the group in terms of the benefits to them from their participation.

Variations on this could be where a researcher conceives of an intervention, such as participation in a support group, but works to cultivate joint leadership and design with the participants (see, for example, Maguire, 1993). These examples assume the researcher is not organic to the group under study, but is offering services or an intervention to them, perhaps for mutual benefit. Data gathering in these cases is documentation of the process and the outcomes. In addition, as stated previously, the researcher will want to keep track, through a researcher's journal, of the various decisions made, self-reflections, and so forth. Data analysis takes place throughout the data-gathering process and informs the ongoing intervention.

As we have discussed previously, it is not uncommon for doctoral students to be part of a larger research or evaluation effort, perhaps funded by a grant or community group. Students, such as Mock (1999), discussed in Chapter 6, often delineate a study within the larger study that is their piece for the dissertation research. In cases such as these, the doctoral student will want to have a sense of the overall data-gathering process and see how much of that is helpful for their dissertation piece; this will also let them get a sense of what other data they will specifically want to pursue. Students will also want to negotiate agreements early on as to the use of the larger data set and their access to it for dissertation and publication purposes; this is particularly important when students are perhaps employed for the larger research initiative—that is, as part of their jobs they are to gather data that contributes to the larger project.

An outside researcher may be invited to participate in an initiative that insiders want to set in motion and study; often, the outsider offers expertise in research methods that the local community may or may not see as its expertise. In these kinds of studies, there are many variations of the working relationships: insiders and outsiders both develop the research questions and the data-gathering methodologies, one group may have more say than the other or both have equal say, and the research addresses the goals of both or of the local group. See chapter 3 and Bartunek and Louis (1996) for a fuller accounting of these possibilities.

A careful negotiating and establishing of trusted relationships is probably the key ingredient in building a research endeavor that works for all involved. For the researcher wanting to use this kind of arrangement for dissertation purposes, it is imperative that issues such as who owns the data and who can disseminate findings and conclusions be negotiated upfront and early on. This is even more complicated if the doctoral student is being employed as an outside consultant for purposes of conducting the research. Ideally, the "research addresses the goals of both parties" (Bartunek & Louis, 1996, p. 25)—that is, it serves the needs of the community seeking the action research, and doctoral students see a melding of these goals with those of their own research.

Early on in the working relationship, time primarily must go to framing the focus of the research and agreeing on the research questions. This is done on at least two levels: listening intently to community concerns and issues that will be addressed through the action research, and then, in this context, framing the doctoral student's research questions. These may or may not be the same. For example, doctoral students assisting with the action research of others may be interested in documenting the realities of forging these kinds of working relationships. This study, then, is a study within the larger action research and may depend primarily on the researcher's journal and the gathering of others' impressions of how the working together evolved. Or, perhaps a doctoral student is working with a community to assess the needs of youth and the effectiveness of community organizations and interventions already in place. Within this large research agenda, it is possible to delineate a strand of study of particular interest to the doctoral student, perhaps through focusing on a particular population—girls or a certain age group or parents' concerns. The data gathered will address both the larger action research study as well as the piece that is the focus for the student's dissertation. Methodologically, then, doctoral students are helping to design the larger research endeavor as well as their own dissertation research.

The Literature Review: Literature in Dialogue With the Data

In action research, there is a conceptual framework that guides the data gathering and analysis, as well as a conceptual framework embedded in one's particular approach to action research. The former is guided by the literature that has been reviewed and the latter by the knowledge interests of the research (Habermas, 1971) discussed in chapter 2. Usually, these frameworks will be compatible in the sense that more utilitarian, functionalist theoretical frameworks usually follow from a technical knowledge interest. More constructivist, interactionist frameworks follow from a practical knowledge interest. And an emancipatory knowledge interest will usually lead to neo-Marxist, feminist, and critical race theories. Most PAR has an emancipatory knowledge interest, whereas, for instance, much action research aimed at organizational development has some combination of a technical and practical knowledge interest.

We made the case earlier that the methodology will continue to develop and shift as the researcher pursues the spirals of action research. We suggest that the literature drawn on for the study will develop as the researcher grows into a deeper understanding of the issues under study. Typically, action research is pursued with iterative cycles of plan-act-observe-reflect (Lewin, 1948); this process is done in relation to a larger body of literature that helps illuminate the findings, deepen the understanding, and perhaps suggest directions for the next iteration. We see a dialogue of sorts taking place between the researcher's growing observations and data and what others have written and understood about similar questions or contexts. The end result should be that the data analysis is pushed by relevant literature and the literature should be extended through the contribution of this action research. This latter point is important to underscore, because action research has often been seen as solely a contribution to local knowledge and practice rather than to the knowledge bases of the various disciplines.

Researchers should expect that as the cycles of research illuminate the issues being studied, new literature will be incorporated as part of this growing understanding. We find that, typically, there is a sense of unearthing the real issues or questions for study, and this often leads researchers to read in directions that they had not previously anticipated. Analysis of the data should be ongoing, as should the review of the literature. As with the methodology section, the literature review from the proposal phase is expected to shift and change when written up for the dissertation.

Writing the Dissertation

While much of action research can be collaborative, signified by intense, ongoing relationships, the actual writing of a dissertation—action research or otherwise—is typically an individual undertaking. It is also not unusual that the same participants who are quite involved in the decision making and meaning making throughout the research process, who have posed questions that are of vital interest to them, may not be interested in writing up the project for public dissemination or as a contribution to the larger literature. This occurs partly because the rewards for the hard work of writing and disseminating the knowledge gained through the inquiry more typically follow an academic career than that of a practitioner or community member; specifically, in the case of writing up dissertation research, the motive for the doctoral student is clear while not so obvious for other participants in the inquiry process. What is not uncommon, though, is a form of member checking (Lincoln & Guba, 1985), where doctoral students present back to the research community the understandings they have come to in the research process. This is commonly done as an ongoing process throughout the research, based on an ongoing analysis that can help guide future actions and research decisions. It is easily folded into the ongoing reflective component of action research, where one is assessing where the efforts thus far have taken the research. While member checking is not to be understood necessarily as gaining community approval, at the same time it recognizes that the process is a collective endeavor. The final written product can only be enriched and made more complex by accounting for varying perspectives based on stakeholders' various positions in the research endeavor. Ultimately, though, it is the doctoral student's understanding that is presented and defended to the academic community.

Because of the ongoing nature of action research, it may not be possible to write up the whole undertaking, but rather just a piece of the understanding or intervention that has come about through the inquiry. The doctoral student may be well aware that the inquiry continues to unfold but may make the decision to write up just a part of it for the dissertation. It is not that the research is finished; rather, the doctoral student bounds it for purposes of the dissertation. This results in a document that is essentially an accounting of the research thus far.

Battaglia (1995), a staff developer for a large, inner-city school district in western New York, discusses her struggles with writing her dissertation and subsequent publications from it.

About midway through this project, I wrote a journal entry where I described Action Research as being "confused, but on a higher level and about more important things!" As I documented the events and the thinking of this project in preparation for publication, I realize that there is much truth in that statement. As I write, I find that my attempt to distill experience into words is frustrating, difficult, trying, and agonizing. One fails more than one succeeds. The words that come and offer themselves as expressions never quite seem to capture my experiences. The experiences always seem just beyond the reach of words. And yet, words are the tools we use as the primary means of expressing experience. It is a challenge, and one that I know is never completely met. My words are, therefore, always provisional, incomplete, partial. (p. 90)

Some have asked whether action research studies have findings, since reports of action research often tend to focus more on process. Students should not be surprised to have committee members unfamiliar with action research ask, "So, what are your findings?" Here the implication is often that they want a concise explanation presented as propositional knowledge of the findings. The idea that knowledge—even in the social sciences—converges on findings has been challenged repeatedly. Lindblom (1995) agues that social science research "often moves toward divergence rather than convergence, toward identifying a bevy of possible scenarios rather than one or a few propositions that social scientists might judge to have won a degree of acceptability" (p. 172). This appears to be especially true for action research and has important implications for how findings are reported in dissertations. We are suggesting that solid action research leads to a deepened understanding of the question posed as well as to more sophisticated questions. The findings should demonstrate this kind of deepened understanding, but how the researcher wants to *represent* them is more open. As the researcher is immersed in the analysis of the data, he or she simultaneously wants to be asking what is the most effective means of representing what has been found. The researcher also wants to take into account the audience for the findings (practitioners, policy makers, etc.) and a style of representation that speaks to those being addressed. Qualitative researchers, especially those who do qualitative evaluation studies, have perfected ways to report findings to decision makers that both preserves some sense of the thick description of the setting and provides useful findings (see Patton, 1996, 2001).

Because of the link in action research between the generation of knowledge and social change, many researchers have turned to alternative mediums for the dissemination of knowledge beyond the immediate site. For instance, increasingly, action research dissertations include a video component. Asten (1993) provides an example of such a dissertation (see also Brown, 1993).

This dissertation is an interrelated filmed/written ethnographic study of four lesbian families living in American society. The purpose of this research is to examine intimate relationships within lesbian families. There are two parts to the study: (1) the production of an ethnographic film through participant observation and feminist participatory research; and (2) a written analysis/report to accompany the film. This study considers lesbian families from an insider's point of view, and asks several different questions. How are relationships within a lesbian family formed and how do they function? How is "family" defined for these particular four lesbian families? What are the special concerns and/or problems for lesbian families? What are the positive things each person gains from growing up in a lesbian family? What shapes do motherhood and parenthood take in a lesbian family? There are four ethnographic stories within the video. The first story examines a single lesbian mother and her two teenage children. The focus of this story is on the relationship between the mother and her children, the ex-partners and how they have impacted the children, and the children's view on growing up with a lesbian parent. The second story examines the co-parent and her interactions with the children, her partner and the ex-husband. The third story examines the relationships between the biological mother, her oldest daughter and the mother's partner. The fourth story examines the couple's relationship, how they feel about each other and their motherhood, their relationship with their daughter, and the concept of a child having two moms. Finally, this study demonstrates how the use of video can be integrated with the written word to produce scholarly material, so that a visual as well as a written language for lesbian families can begin to take shape. (Asten, 1993, p. 4)

The participatory study described in the next chapter (Mock, 1999) also included a video component. Researchers and community members created videos of interviews with community leaders to use internally for future professional development. The use of videos will require additional permissions from participants and IRB approval.

Defending the Dissertation

The dissertation defense is an important ritual of academic life that varies somewhat from campus to campus. Most dissertation defenses are open to the public, and therefore it is appropriate for the participants of a dissertation study to attend. Some believe that a dissertation defense is strictly an academic exercise between the student and his or her dissertation committee and not a participatory venue. They argue that there are other, more appropriate forums for sharing and/or negotiating findings with participants of action research studies. Some participants might attend for moral support, but would not want to participate in the questions or discussion.

Another view is that the defense of the dissertation is a good litmus test of how participatory the research has been or, at least, to what extent participants feel they are portrayed evenhandedly. Even students who have had minimal collaboration with participants should have engaged in member checking throughout the research process and certainly well before a dissertation defense—that is, participants should be presented with the study's findings and have an opportunity to provide feedback.

In more participatory studies, the findings are seldom a surprise to participants. In fact, participants who have attended dissertation defenses have been known to jump to the student's defense if he or she is questioned harshly by committee members. In such cases, participants feel a sense of ownership in the dissertation even if they did not participate in the written product. Once again, the decision of how to structure the defense of an action research dissertation will depend on how participatory the study was and how open the dissertation committee is to having participants formally involved in the process. Some committees view the defense of the dissertation as largely a celebration that occurs once everyone has agreed it is in final form. Others see the defense as providing final feedback with the real possibility that major revisions may yet need to be done. The local culture of the university and committee concerning the function of the defense will also determine how it is structured. Typically, faculty set aside between 1 and 2 hours for a dissertation defense and thus an elaborate participatory panel, while desirable, may not be practical in many cases. Scheduling the defense becomes problematic as not only faculty but also participants must be available at the same time. Such a panel would be an excellent way to demonstrate democratic validity as well as provide a venue that is congruent with the spirit of most action research approaches, and should be pursued where feasible.

6

What Does an Action Research Dissertation Look Like?

In this chapter, we provide an in-depth look at two participatory action research (PAR) dissertations and one insider action research dissertation in progress. Our intent is not to provide exemplars, since dissertations will vary widely in their content, style, and organization. But we believe it is useful to see how others who have written action research dissertations have gone about their decision-making process. (For more summaries of action research studies, see chapters 3 and 4 of Anderson, Herr, & Nihlen, 1994.)

The first example is perhaps as close to the middle of the continuum of positionality in chapter 3 as it is possible to be. It resembles in many ways what Bartunek and Louis (1996) call an insider/outsider team. However, while the study is a relatively pure example of PAR, the dissertation itself is relatively traditional in its tone and format, using mixed (qualitative and quantitative) methods. Because much PAR is funded by external agencies and involves teams of researchers and/or evaluators, some dissertations result from doctoral students' participation on these projects. Lynne Mock was a doctoral student who joined a PAR research team and figured out how to carve out her own dissertation from pieces of the larger study as well as pieces she created herself. All PAR dissertations will have to struggle with the collaborative nature of the research and the individual nature of the dissertation.[6]

Because Mock's (1999) dissertation involves both collaboration and ongoing cycles of action, it captures the essence of PAR, as well as demonstrates how PAR projects can result in dissertation studies. Several scenarios are possible for a PAR dissertation: (a) a doctoral student seeks out a group or agency with whom to do participatory research (see Maguire, 1987a, 1993); (b) a practitioner in an organization, who is also a doctoral student, initiates or joins a participatory research project with outside researchers and/or other insiders; or (c) a doctoral student joins a participatory action research project and participates as an outsider, usually under the supervision of a faculty member. Mock's dissertation illustrates the last scenario, while Alice McIntyre's (1995) study, described in the subsequent section, is an example of the first.

McIntyre's (1995) dissertation, also published as a book in 1997, is a less "pure" attempt at PAR in the sense that it is further toward the outsider end of the positionality continuum. McIntyre brought together a group of student teachers with an agenda that was not negotiated with the group itself. It is typical of many PAR dissertations in which an outside researcher initiates a participatory research group with the goal of deepening understandings and moving to action. This type of group research is often centered on catalytic and democratic validity (chapter 4) and aims at an emancipatory knowledge interest (Habermas, 1971). It qualifies as PAR because group members were involved in other phases of the research, such as data analysis, and because participants' understandings of their beliefs and practices were deepened and several were moved to action. Stylistically, the dissertation represents a more qualitative, narrative approach.

John Mark Dyke's work is an example of insider action research. A full-time employee in Child Protective Services (CPS), his research grew out of issues he and others were facing in the bureaucracy. We include it because, as we have previously described, issues of action research vary according to the researcher's positionality. In Dyke's case, he is an insider to the organization, occupying multiple roles as an employee as well as a researcher. Beyond insider action research, it is also an example of a trend we are noticing where doctoral students begin to pilot their research and these pilots lead into the dissertation research. The dissertation, then, is the latest piece of research work in a series. We are interested in this because action research is so time consuming. The pilot work is one way to begin the research process and document how it unfolds and leads to the dissertation research. Dyke's work also is in keeping with the idea that insider action research can be a more authentic response to outside initiatives or guidelines (in this case, federal policy) that impose improvement plans on organizations.

Lynne Mock: Carving a Dissertation out of a PAR Project

Lynne Mock was a master's student at the University of Illinois at Chicago (UIC) at the time the PAR project began in 1990. She ultimately did both her master's thesis and her doctoral dissertation in community psychology as part of this research team, which was led by James Kelly, a professor in community psychology and long-time practitioner and advocate of participatory research. Dr. Kelly and several graduate students worked with a church-based community-organizing group, the Developing Communities Project (DCP), to document the development of African American community leaders in the Chicago south side community where DCP is located.

Whereas this PAR project represented nonconventional research in social science terms—particularly for a psychology department—Mock's dissertation drew on some fairly traditional qualitative and quantitative research methods. Furthermore, unlike some PAR dissertations that have a more self-reflective, narrative style, this one is an articulate and intelligently written, but concise exposition of the research. We selected this example in part because it is well documented through publications that contextualize the study and provide accounts of behind-the-scenes decision making, and because we believe that many students who do action research dissertations may have fairly traditional committees. Thus, as we cautioned in chapter 5, it is wise to view the dissertation as in part a political document that is written—like all writing—for a particular audience. What might be acceptable and even encouraged in an avant-garde women's studies program might not fly in a traditional department of psychology.

The number of university faculty capable of guiding a student through a path-breaking PAR dissertation are few, and in some fields nonexistent. In fact, many students do action research dissertations without any particular recognition on the part of the student or committee members that their research departs radically from both traditional quantitative and qualitative research. Such dissertations, as we described in chapter 3, can end up positioning the researcher in an awkward outsider-within status in which a full examination of the inside/outside and collaborative tensions in the research are ignored or sidestepped.

As mentioned above, the project was chosen in part because of the amount of formal and informal documentation that existed (Kelly, 1999; Kelly et al., 2004; Kelly, Mock, & Tandon, 2001; Tandon, Kelly, & Mock, 2001). The genesis of this project was a funding grant that the DCP was seeking that contained an evaluation component. James Kelly describes how this occurred:

> A staff member . . . of a State Agency (Department of Alcoholism and Substance Abuse) phoned in the fall of 1989 to inquire of my interest to evaluate a substance abuse proposal in an African-American community. The then Director of the Agency . . . had been employing the ecological framework in training prevention staff. [She] thought that I might be an appropriate resource for this work. I thought that this might be an opportunity to do just what I really wanted to do: to be connected to citizen leadership development and to create a research site for doctoral students in community psychology. (Kelly et al., 2004, p. 206)

The DCP would receive $150,000 a year for community organizing activities, with an extra $50,000 for an evaluation component. A meeting was set up with Department of Alcoholism and Substance abuse staff, the director and associate director of DCP, and Dr. Kelly. The following is Dr. Kelly's account of the meeting:

> I made two points at the meeting: First, it is a mistake to devote time and energy to evaluate community organizing efforts by imposing various experimental designs and thereby think that one could assess and/or control the multiple factors that impact a diminution of the use of substances at the community level. An alternative evaluation approach could concentrate on documenting community members who were being trained and developed as community leaders by the organization. The premise would be that a community that has competent and well-organized participants could in turn mobilize substantial community efforts and resources to reduce social problems in their own community. Second, if I was to be involved, I would hope that the work could be collaborative, in that all decisions about evaluation methods and procedures would be a process of joint decision making between the DCP participants and UIC. The DCP staff seemed surprised and positive about my approach. (Kelly et al., 2004, p. 207)

THE ENTRY PROCESS

According to Dick (2000), a PAR dissertation should make clear how entry into the client system was negotiated and how structures were set up for participation. PAR depends on a careful initial building of relationships and negotiation of roles, often referred to as the entry process. Dr. Kelly describes how he worked to gain the confidence of the DCP staff in subsequent encounters. Community organizations are busy places and meetings are difficult to set up. After several failed attempts at face-to-face meetings and a few phone conversations, a face-to-face encounter with the DCP executive director, John Owens, became a key event in the entry process. It is important to know that Dr. Kelly was a white professor at the local flagship public university. John Owens was an African American with roots in the local community, likely somewhat skeptical of "ivory tower" academics. Dr. Kelly describes the encounter:

> John Owens volunteered to come to my office at the University. On my office door was a picture of Max Roach, Jazz drummer. . . . John seemed shocked and/or amazed. Then he smiled and said "Kelly, you can't be all bad." He was an avid jazz fan. Our conversation that afternoon was animated. Before we discussed our work together we must have spent twenty minutes discussing our favorite jazz musicians and CDs. He had a dinner meeting in downtown Chicago so in departing the university I accompanied him and left him at his restaurant. This was the "ice breaker" event in the entry process. (Kelly et al., 2004, p. 207)

We present this example of an entry process because participatory research often requires a considerable amount of time and effort to establish rapport among participants. In this case, not only did organizational and status differences need to be negotiated, but a white academic had to be viewed as credible and trustworthy by an activist African American community organization. While Lynne Mock, who later produced a dissertation from this study, was not involved at this stage of entry, many doctoral students will essentially find themselves in Dr. Kelly's shoes, needing to build credibility with participants. (See Maguire, 1987b, 1993, for an account of this process from a doctoral student's perspective.)

Even a doctoral student entering the process after formal entry has been negotiated must establish credibility with participants in order to work effectively as a participatory researcher. Furthermore, if entry has not been effectively negotiated, a doctoral student will find it difficult to gather authentic data. Mock, who was the only African American on the university research team, discusses these tensions:

> When Sandra interviewed me in the fall of 1990, I expressed concerns about how I would be perceived on the project. I started out with a lot of questions and concerns. Being the only African-American on the project, would I be perceived as a token on the project? Will I be perceived as a "collaborator" in the negative sense—a black person working for the university and exploiting the black community? Was the evaluation requested by the community organization or required of them? Over time, I learned that I would be valued for my growing expertise in our work and for my experiences as an African-American woman. The main difference between myself and the members of the panel was my formal training in psychology. Although the evaluation was required, the organization did have a choice in who would be conducting the evaluation and how it would be done. Everyone was very positive about our collaborative approach to documenting the work of the organization. (Kelly et al., 2004, p. 211)

Villenas (1996) has also described the dilemmas of scholars of color who are associated with dominant institutions as they do research within communities of color. These complex issues of boundary crossing should be discussed at length in action research dissertations, because the trustworthiness of the data depends on effectively negotiating entry and building rapport with participants. In Mock's case, she was an outsider to this particular community but, as an African American, was in some respects more of an insider than her non–African American research colleagues.

CREATING PARTICIPATORY STRUCTURES

Shortly after his meeting with John Owens, Dr. Kelly met with the DCP board and recommended they appoint a DCP-UIC liaison person who would advise on the style and substance of the work, facilitate data collection, and interpret the needs of the DCP community to the university group and vice versa. While the liaison would be an important conduit of information and socialization, a more representative group was needed to make the project truly participatory. John Owens composed an eight-person community research panel made up of DCP members who would meet with the UIC group to decide on what topics should be documented and what methods should be used. The panel included a parent, a Catholic elementary school principal, a welfare rights advocate, a public school principal, a community organization executive, a labor organizer, a citizen active in school reform, and a pastor. At this point, two graduate students, Cecile Lardon, in community psychology, and Lynne Mock, in clinical psychology, agreed to work on the project. Ultimately, four master's theses and two doctoral dissertations resulted from this PAR project.

The following quote from Mock's (1999) dissertation discusses the importance of participatory structures for the collaboration of participants in all stages of the study.

> The author, in conjunction with a team of researchers from the University of Illinois at Chicago worked in collaboration with a Community Research Panel (CRP) and an Action Task Force (ATF) (Kelly, 1992; in press). The CRP was created in 1990 when the executive director of DCP was asked to recommend eight citizens of various backgrounds: The Community Research Panel (CRP) was an invaluable resource for helping the author and other UIC researchers define goals and methods for documenting community leadership development. The CRP critically evaluated research concepts and topics presented by the UIC researchers for the documentation, and also, recommended new themes, concepts, and topics to be addressed (Glidewell, Kelly, Bagby, and Dickerson, 1998; Mock, 1994; Kelly, 1992; 1993).
>
> This research also affirms a concept of emerging importance in community psychology: collaborative research methods (Tyler, Pargament, & Glanz, 1983; Whyte, 1986;1989; Kingry-Westergaard & Kelly, 1986; Greenwood, Whyte, & Harkavy, 1993). The direction of this study was further stimulated by discussions with members of the Community Research Panel (CRP) who were consulted during the conceptualization of this project. Ideally, the involvement of community residents and leaders would increase the utility of the research for the participants and others in the setting (Chavis, Stucky, & Wandersman, 1983; Whyte, 1986; 1989; Kingry-Westergaard & Kelly, 1986; Greenwood, Whyte, & Harkavy, 1993). DCP is in the process of planning to use these research findings in the future training of DCP leaders (Kelly, in press).
>
> The Action Task Force (ATF) was created in 1997 to collaborate with the research team on the interpretation and utility of the data collected for the larger study (including Study 1 and 2 described below). The ATF consists of ten DCP leaders nominated by the current executive director, and is chaired by the UIC DCP liaison who is also the secretary of the DCP Board of Directors. Nine meetings, including a retreat, have been held to date culminating in recommendations to the DCP Board regarding specific actions to be taken based on the research data, for example, the creation of leadership training materials. (pp. 30–31)

These panels and task forces made up of agency and community members participated in every phase of the research. It is important for a dissertation to make clear the degree of collaboration with participants. In chapter 4, we discussed catalytic validity of action research, particularly when it is participative. PAR is valid in this sense to the extent that the research is educative for all parties and stimulates some action. Limiting participation to the initial stages of a project or merely involving them at the end to validate findings reduces the catalytic validity of the research. To the extent that diverse perspectives are not included, it also reduces the study's democratic validity.

Many wonder how collaborative data analysis works in practice. Tandon, Kelly, and Mock (2001) provide an in-depth discussion of how participants collaborated in data gathering and analysis.

> Because this process was labor intensive, the UIC research team did not ask DCP members to assist in coding the eighty interviews. Cognizant of the time demands placed upon DCP staff, board, and members, the UIC research team felt that continuous dialogue with the DCP executive director and the UIC/DCP liaison person was a more prudent approach in discussing the initial data analysis. The executive director and liaison person actively undertook two responsibilities.
>
> First, they examined each of the sixty codes for clarity. Specifically, they reviewed codes' definitions and suggested alternative wordings to accurately reflect the nature of the codes in the larger context of DCP. Second, the codes were examined for their potential relevance and utility for DCP. Further, the executive director and liaison person identified codes of particular interest to DCP. Codes relating to DCP's church-based organization were among those strongly supported by DCP's executive director, as she was interested in understanding the role that religion had in the work of DCP members.
>
> Working with DCP's executive director and liaison person, we created a set of fifty-six mutually agreed upon codes. Thus, DCP and the UIC research team jointly shaped the building blocks for future data analysis and interpretation. Furthermore, these preliminary data analysis steps attempted to acknowledge both parties' unique skills and expertise. UIC research team members were responsible for the technical aspects of generating codes from interview transcripts, as they were more skilled in executing data analytic techniques; DCP members employed their knowledge about the host organization and the potential utility to clarify and refine various codes.
>
> The underlying importance of the data analysis stage of PAR is to stimulate research participants' thinking about the potential utility of collected data. The degree to which participants are involved in the actual mechanical aspects of coding interviews or running statistical analyses will vary across projects, but the notion that research participants should understand key findings and their relevance is central. (p. 205)

A member of the UIC research team also prepared a quote book with examples of quotes of interviewees that represented the various codes. This provided a better sense to participants of the relevance and meaning of the codes. The team also prepared tree-shaped data displays that grouped codes into five general themes of community leadership. The quote book and the data displays facilitated further data analysis and discussion with participants.

Data analysis is often the final stage of most research, but because PAR is action oriented, a community action task force was formed to discuss how this data could inform next steps.

> At an all day meeting in November 1997 several concrete proposals were made to increase the visibility of the findings within the DCP community. Examples were for every church to create a DCP Newsletter and a brochure for recruiting. Follow up discussions with sub groups of the Action Task Force reemphasized how the data could contribute to training needs. In the spring of 1998 at meetings of sub groups of the Action Task Force DCP participants gave anecdotes about events that should be captured and included in training materials. It was at this point that I mentioned the possible benefit of oral histories as a resource, particularly if they were videotaped. There was enthusiasm for this idea. The Action Force Task Members believed that the videos could be used for fund raising as well as training. Some believed that they could also provide a history of DCP. (Tandon, Kelly, & Mock, 2001, p. 207)

Videos of six DCP leaders were produced with an edited version with selections from each of the six individual videos. Although Lynne Mock was part of this multiyear research process from shortly after entry, her work as part of the research team and her data gathering for her dissertation proceeded on parallel and often overlapping tracks. The results of the collaboratively gathered qualitative data formed the basis for the largely individual develop-ment of the Personal Vision Scale (PVS) that became the centerpiece of her dissertation.

WRITING THE DISSERTATION

This section will not systematically summarize the findings of Lynne Mock's dissertation, which can be accessed through Dissertation Abstracts. Our interest is in how a doctoral student who participated in a PAR project crafted a dissertation out of a collaborative research effort. The primary audi-ence of a dissertation is a committee, made up of faculty with particular disci-plinary backgrounds and expectations of what a dissertation should look like. Mock's academic program consisted of both clinical and community psychol-ogy, two subfields of psychology with very different research traditions. In a methodologically conservative field like psychology, Mock needed to construct a dissertation that would look fairly traditional, while justifying the kind of collaborative approach more characteristic of community psychology than other subfields.

Mock's (1999) dissertation actually consists of three studies. She contributed to the qualitative, descriptive part of the study but also incorporated a more individual component in which she validated her PVS and compared DCP leaders with a sample of community residents.

The first study employed semi-structured interviews to explore the content and structure of community leaders' personal visions, related goals, and circumstances under which personal visions are discussed. The second study, using a subsample of community leaders from the first study, sought to provide further support for the construct validity of the Personal Vision Scale (PVS). The PVS assesses the visioning process with the assumption that visioning occurs in three developmental phases. The third study employed questionnaires and the PVS to contrast the personal vision content, structure, and PVS scores of DCP leaders and a sample of community residents. (p. xi)

Her review of the literature was done in a separate chapter and in a traditional manner. (For a good resource on writing a literature review, see Hart, 1998.) She reviewed the literature on visionary and transformational leadership, as well as literature on leadership scale development. While notions of visionary and transformative leadership are popular, they are also very complex concepts that vary from context to context. Drawing on the experience of a visionary such as Martin Luther King and the grassroots movement he helped to create, Mock (1999) sought to understand how local communities developed these qualities in their members. She ended the review by calling for more studies of leadership in community-based organizations, such as the one she was studying.

Community work and social change is reflected in the history of the African-American community (Morris, 1984; Payne, 1995), yet there exists a dearth of systematic, empirical study of these processes. As Dr. Martin Luther King stated during his 1968 address to the Society for the Psychological Study of Social Issues, there is much to be learned about the process of social change (1968). Dr. King urged psychologists to study, understand, and facilitate the process in this area (Kelly, in press; American Psychologist Association, 1999). It is hoped that this work is able to shed some light on the process of social change by understanding the development of community leaders and their visions for community change. (p. 26)

She also argues later in her dissertation for further studies of leadership in African American communities, particularly studies that do not pathologize these communities.

Leadership among African American citizens is a neglected area of study. Even in Bass's comprehensive volume on leadership, the information on African Americans and other people of color seemed inadequate (1990). No empirical studies of merit were cited. In this topic of study, longitudinal, multi-method studies are needed to better understand and facilitate community leadership development in the African American adults reporting different levels of visioning, activism, volunteerism, and commitment to community institutions. Leadership behaviors such as visioning, goal setting, vision implementation, group discussion and mobilization were described. This area of research should be further expanded and explored, particularly the impact of emotions and religious beliefs on commitment to community work. (pp. 80–81)

This research is among the growing number of psychological studies that has a non-pathological focus on African-American adult behavior (White, 1991; Guthrie, 1991). In this study, African Americans adults were described as future-oriented, resourceful, active, and concerned about their community. These leaders were supported by African American church institutions involved in community work, and personal and community development. These data provide further evidence that African Americans are thoughtful, concerned, and active; and, continue to pursue personal development in adulthood. African Americans work and struggle together, exert influence, have collective power, and care deeply about their communities. DCP is an example of an African American setting that helps individuals address oppression and exclusion from the broader society. Within DCP, these individuals are able to voice their community concerns. Also, DCP is an action-oriented setting that provides training and opportunities for development. In addition, because the context is church-based, religious values are affirmed and put into action through their community work. More research on the many types of normative behaviors of African American adults is needed in psychology. (pp. 81–82)

EMPHASIZING THE STRENGTHS OF ACTION RESEARCH

A key strategy for action research dissertations is to take what some might consider a limitation and turn it into an advantage. This was an early strategy of qualitative researchers who argued that they could provide the kind of "thick description" (Geertz, 1983) of local reality that the much thinner, but generalizable data of most quantitative research could not provide. While this is not a crucial issue for Mock, as she uses both qualitative and quantitative analyses, she must justify a collaborative approach to research that some academics may find problematic. Unlike traditional research, action research produces knowledge grounded in local realities that is also useful to local participants. Epistemologies and methodologies that involve participants and are capable of responding to local realities and needs are sometimes insufficiently appreciated in the academy.

In the following section of her dissertation, Mock draws on Kingry-Westergaard and Kelly's (1986) notion of *contextualist epistemology* to argue for the appropriateness of her methodology to the experience and needs of the participants. This notion is very close to democratic or ecological validity discussed in chapter 4:

Unfortunately, there exists a dearth of psychological research on African Americans that is normative in nature (Guthree, 1991; Akbar, 1991). According to advocates of African American psychology, research should be useful to the African American community, providing an understanding of normal behavior, and/or providing solutions in problem-solving oriented research (White, 1991; Guthrie, 1991; Akbar; 1991; Bowman, 1991). To insure the usefulness of the research for the African American community, participants should have significant involvement in the research

(Bowman, 1991). Also, the research enterprise must be relevant to the needs and the experiences of the community. It is also important that community members have a role and a voice in the research (Akbar, 1991; Bowman, 1991). When the research is complete, the results should be disseminated to the community in understandable and useful ways. (Akbar, 1991; Guthrie, 1991).

Consistent with views of several African American psychologists, several community psychologists promote a "contextualist epistemology" which assumes that knowledge exists within a specific empirical and theoretical frame of reference (Kingry-Westergaard & Kelly, 1986). Also, contextualism assumes that the research is embedded in the world the researcher observes. Researchers are responsible for selecting and justifying their empirical and theoretical structures and are encouraged to select complimentary methodologies in their research (Kingry-Westergaard & Kelly, 1986). Robust, contextualist research includes analyses of the discriminant and convergent validity of the concepts under study. The use of multiple methods and analyses compensate for each other's limitations and contribute to understanding concepts and phenomena. Methods are influenced by the interests, values, and assumptions of the researcher (Kingry-Westergaard & Kelly, 1986). A collaborative approach to methodology is valued where the observer and the observed develop a reciprocal learning relationship. Several persons in the setting under study are assumed to have knowledge and expertise valuable to the research enterprise. Their input, and the dialogue between researchers and research participants is expected to enhance the authenticity and utility of the research findings (Kingry-Westergaard & Kelly, 1986; Kelly, 1992). I believe that this approach is invaluable in exploratory and preliminary studies.

This research was guided by a contextualist methodological approach. The focus is on leadership among African American adults with an aim to increase understanding of leadership behaviors in a church-based community coalition. Representatives of the participants in this study have been involved in the larger research program from its inception through various disseminations: publications (Glidewell et al., 1997; Tandon et al., 1998), presentations, and preliminary reports. Also, this particular work employs a combination of qualitative and quantitative data analyses to explore, in depth, the concept of personal vision among African American, church-based, community leadership. (pp. 6–7)

We think this study is a model of good PAR, but we also realize that Mock's study may seem intimidating to many students starting out on an action research dissertation. This was a well-funded study that occurred over nearly a decade. Mock's use of mixed methods and her three studies makes it seem almost like multiple dissertations. She also spent several years working with the project, while doing her master's thesis and doctoral dissertation, enjoying the mentorship of a professor and a team of colleagues who worked with her throughout this time.

Most doctoral students have neither the availability of such a funded PAR study nor the methodological preparation to do a quality mixed-methods study. The following smaller-scale study by Alice McIntyre may be more typical of PAR dissertations.

Alice McIntyre: Initiating a PAR Group

Because not all doctoral students have ongoing PAR projects they can join, many must initiate their own studies. These studies often involve researchers working collaboratively with a group to both better understand a social phenomena (e.g., teen pregnancy, domestic violence, professional dilemmas, etc.) and also deepen participants' understandings and leading to some kind of action or advocacy to address the issue. Patricia Maguire (1987a) initiated a support and research group of battered women; Elizabeth Saavedra (1994) facilitated a teacher inquiry group; Tammy Ann Schwartz (2002) met regularly with a group of urban Appalachian girls from her old neighborhood.[6] There are many excellent dissertations that have resulted from these self-initiated, participatory studies, and we have chosen to describe one by Alice McIntyre (1995) that was also published as a book (McIntyre, 1997a), *Making Meaning of Whiteness: Exploring Racial Identity With White Teachers.*

As we discussed in the previous example, the negotiation of access is a key issue in PAR, and James Kelly spent considerable time on this phase of the study to assure a reasonable level of reciprocity between the university researchers and the participants. McIntyre (1997a) is honest about the fact the she entered the study with an interest in teachers' white racial identity. This was not a burning issue—to say the least—for her participants, who were largely unaware of their racial identities in or out of the classroom. In the following passage, McIntyre (1997a) reflects on why she chose to enter the study with an "agenda" and why she nevertheless justifies PAR as her methodology.

> A recurring question in the PAR literature is whether the researcher needs to be requested as a resource by a community or group, or whether the researcher can determine that a problem exists and then decide to engage with a group in a participatory approach to solving it. I chose the latter approach and entered this study recognizing that there were many predetermined aspects of this research that seem antithetical to the overall methodological stance of a PAR project. Whereas some PAR projects involve joint research designs between the participants and the researcher, the very fact that this was a dissertation proposal initiated by me and that it was contingent on institutional approval—prior to investigation and action— make that specific step problematic. Notwithstanding, I pursued the project because of my belief in the underlying tenets of PAR: (1) an emphasis on the lived experiences of human beings, (2) the subjectivity and activist stance of the researcher, and (3) an emphasis on social change. (p. 21)

Because of the emancipatory goals of most PAR, many beginning researchers find it attractive but also intimidating. McIntyre found many apparent contradictions in her research, such as imposing the agenda and working with members of the dominant racial group rather than an oppressed group. This is normal. Almost all researchers using PAR express doubts about the "purity" of their projects, but it is important to remember that all research has limitations. Honesty is the best policy in such cases, but it is also necessary to explain why these limitations are not fatal to the study. In fact, this reflexivity about one's role in the research is a key characteristic of all forms of action research.

It should be said, however, that so-called participatory research that is excessively impositional or that cynically uses the appearance of participation to impose an agenda is not acceptable. McIntyre (1997a) discusses how these concerns emerged early in her research:

> I attended a PAR conference with a group of academics, graduate students, community activists, educators, and social workers while I was in the initial stages of my dissertation. During our 2-day meeting, we engaged in many heated and informative debates about what constitutes "participation" in a PAR project, what is the meaning of "research" in PAR, and how does one define "action" in a PAR project? There were a range of responses to the questions we articulated and we found ourselves reconfiguring combinations of the three aspects of PAR—participation, research, and action—in ways that challenged our assumptions about the "right" way to do PAR. We discovered that there are multiple ways of designing a PAR project just as there are multiple ways of addressing the distinctive challenges that emerge out of and through actual PAR experiences.
>
> For me, in particular, I encountered a set of issues that challenged me to think about the cooptation of PAR within a university setting. I grappled with questions of ownership, coanalysis, power relations with both my dissertation committee and the research participants, and the larger issue of who, exactly, was going to benefit from this project? I wanted to see this work as "part of a larger discourse on emancipatory, liberatory, or transformative practice" (Hall, 1993, p. xiv), yet, oftentimes felt constrained by the complexities of conducting PAR with a privileged group of white females in a university setting, *and* by my occasional feelings of self-doubt concerning the "purity" of this project.
>
> Yet, I was also excited about the idea of engaging in an alternative research methodology for examining whiteness, and was enthusiastic about the prospect of "breaking new ground" in an educational setting that oftentimes gets comfortable with complacency. The PAR methodology attracted me. And the attraction *to* was greater than the fear *of*. (p. 23)

McIntyre's (1997a) data consisted of initial, semistructured, 1-hour interviews with each of 13 participants, followed by eight group sessions, lasting 2 hours each. During these sessions, they discussed readings and shared personal stories and teaching experiences related to the subject of race. All interviews and sessions were audiotaped, transcribed, and presented to the participants for their feedback prior to and during data analysis. She describes how the groups were run:

I was a participant, a coordinator, and a researcher in these sessions. I also facilitated many of the conversations, cognizant of the fact that the need to discuss the lived experiences of the participants is a central tenet of PAR. I began each session with a brief overview of the previous session inviting comments, clarifications, or both from the participants. Following this introduction, I either suggested that we take up a question or an issue raised from previous conversations, or, I requested that the participants join in an activity related to the research topic. For example, after 3 weeks of discussing various definitions of racism and sharing a myriad of personal stories about race, racism, and being white, I asked the participants during the session four to create collages that represented whiteness. (p. 26)

The abstract of her dissertation is worth studying since it contains most aspects of her study: (a) details about her participants, (b) goals of the study, (c) the basic design of the study, (d) positionality of the researcher, (e) PAR methodology, and (f) implications of research for teacher education.

This participatory action research project explored the meaning of Whiteness, and White racial identity, with 13 White middle- and upper middle-class female student teachers at a private northeastern university. This project (1) examined what it means for the participants to be White, (2) analyzed ways of making meaning about Whiteness, and the participants' difficulties in thinking critically about race and racism, and (3) explored the implications of the participants' racial identities in the formulation of their teaching practices. During eight group discussions, ways of constructing Whiteness were created, problematized and critiqued. The group sessions were organized around a theme, a question, an activity, an experience the students had at their field sites, a problem posed by the researcher or the participants or an idea that emerged from the project itself. Exploring the complexities of racial identity, Whiteness and the participants' perspectives on how to teach to diversity—within multiparty talk—required an analysis that could uncover the concepts, ideas, and beliefs that shaped the myriad of experiences that multiple participants brought to the research project. Social constructionist grounded theory provided an approach to analyzing the data in terms of those complexities by fostering the development of analytic and conceptual constructions of data, and by stressing the active stance and positionality of the researcher as crucial to the interpretation of the data. An overview of the relevant literature concerning multicultural antiracist education and White racial identity is also presented to situate the analysis of the participants' racial identities. The emphasis on the participants' lived experiences, the subjectivity and activist stance of the researcher, and the emphasis on social change are characteristics of this participatory action research project that provoke possibilities for transformative research and educational praxis. In addition, the implications of this research suggest that teacher preparation programs be aggressive in creating strategies for White student teachers to engage in experiences that disrupt the ideology of Whiteness and provoke the development of antiracist pedagogy. (McIntyre, 1995, p. 4)

She does not explicitly list findings for her study in the abstract. As is often the case with PAR, the findings of the study are often difficult to express in propositional form. In her dissertation and book, McIntyre displays and analyzes transcripts of her discussions with the teachers. Findings cluster around several themes: (a) ways white people "talk themselves out of" being responsible for racism, (b) how white people construct their own white racial identity, (c) what it means to be a white teacher and one's role in reproducing dominant discourses, and (d) the teachers' resistance to examining their white racial identities. Findings are discussed in narrative form and with the use of data displays as illustrations, much as in a qualitative research study.

The issue of teacher "resistance" raises an issue that has been widely discussed in writing on critical (Anderson, 1989), feminist (Lather, 1986a), and other forms of activist research, including some traditions of action research (Carr & Kemmis, 1986). Ellsworth's (1989) much-cited critique of critical pedagogy from a feminist perspective discusses the subtle and not-so-subtle ways critical pedagogies can become impositional and verge on indoctrination. Was the teachers' resistance in this study an artifact of the researcher's attempt to impose an agenda, or were the teachers resisting examining their white racial identity and the ways they may reproduce dominant discourses in the classroom? It may be hard to sort these issues out in PAR, but some attempt should be made to reflect on the extent to which the researcher is being true to participatory principles of mutual respect. One can easily fall into quadrant III (We know; They don't know) of the four squares of knowledge discussed in chapter 3.

McIntyre (1995) put several safeguards in place to make sure that her research was not impositional. She chose not to use her own students in this study, thus attenuating, though not totally avoiding, the issues of hierarchy and power common to studies in which administrators or others in a setting study their clients. This is not to say that insiders should not use their own settings for their research, but it is less problematic to do so when the focus of the research is one's own practice rather than the practice of others.

She openly acknowledges that the initial agenda—a highly controversial one for the teachers—was unilaterally determined. Such openness about the study's "limitation" is essential for PAR. She also built in opportunities for collaboration with participants. For example, she allowed students to enroll in an independent study in which they would collaborate with her in the analysis of data. Three of the participants took her up on it. Working side by side with three of the participants in the analysis of data introduced an important element of collaboration at this stage of the study. McIntyre (1997a) reflects on their participation in data analysis.

> The advantages of being able to engage on a deeper level with the data, was that Christine, Michelle, and Julie reread the transcribed sessions, listened to all the tapes, and delved more meaningfully into readings about racism and whiteness. They situated themselves more critically in the discourse, critiquing both their

individual talk, and the talk that was generated by the group. During the group analysis meetings, they made frequent references to the changes they had under-gone in their thinking about whiteness and racism. (p. 142)

While resistance was encountered during the PAR process, McIntyre (1997a) documents how participants' understandings did shift, both during the process and after the formal sessions concluded, establishing the catalytic validity of her study.

At the end of our eight sessions, the campus where this project was developed experienced a level of racial unrest that resulted in the formation of several new undergraduate student groups that were committed to addressing racism within the university. Although many of the participants resisted taking collective action at the culmination of the group sessions, the public identification of racist behav-ior on campus, coupled with the raising of consciousness experienced within the project, led five of the thirteen participants to join in the formation of under-graduate student groups to address racism at the university. Others have spoken to me about insights they have had into their own positionalities as white people since the project ended and how they have been able to "have conversations about race—something I just couldn't do before without feeling uncomfortable" (Marie). (p. 143)

PUBLISHING FROM PAR DISSERTATIONS

McIntyre defended her dissertation in 1995 and produced a book version and an academic article in 1997 (McIntyre, 1997a, 1997b). Because action research dissertations are often written in a more organic fashion, they can require fewer revisions than a traditional academic dissertation. McIntyre embeds her discussion of methodology in her publications, but unique methodologi-cal dilemmas can also often result in publications. For instance, McIntyre's study is an example of "studying up," or doing participatory research with dominant groups rather than nondominant groups. While McIntyre did not—to our knowledge—write this up as a separate topic for a publication or conference presentation, she does discuss the issue in her dissertation and book.

Infusing the principles of PAR with members of the dominant racial group raises important methodological questions: Why would white people want to examine white racism? What investment do white people have in engaging in a critique about a system we benefit from and in? How does being a member of the domi-nant group affect one's commitment to "radical social change"? Questions like these need to be asked, and the answers need to be heard.

It is my experience that the *possibilities* of conducting PAR with the dominant group need to be the focal point of our research. The inherent contradictions need to be acknowledged, but they need not result in researchers *rejecting* PAR as a resource for understanding social problems and for engaging in critical dialogue. Rather, the complexities can be catalytic, challenging white people to reflect on the causes of racism and the system of whiteness "as being rooted in human actions, [thus coming] to realize that things do not have to remain the way they are and that they can engage in actions to transform the reality. Critique thus turns into will to action and action itself" (Park, 1993, pp. 7–8). (McIntyre, 1997a, p. 141)

John Mark Dyke: Insider Action Research

The third example of dissertation work that we offer is an approach that we find increasingly common: an insider doing action research in his own site over the course of his doctoral program. A series of pilot studies leads to the proposal eventually put forward for the dissertation research. It is based on the unfolding research, previously documented through the pilot studies. While there is definitely a new piece of research for the dissertation, it is an outgrowth of the understanding that has come from the research projects carried out previously. Insider action research requires a complex juggling of multiple roles and relationships, which often invites any number of methodological and ethical quandaries. We find, then, that the learning that transpires through multiple pilot studies, conducted in the same site, is both from the analysis of the data as well as from practicing the methodology of insider action research.

Doctoral students may be able to capitalize on class projects that require a pilot study or "practice research" as part of the course requirements to begin their action research. In addition, doctoral students *may* have room in their program of studies for an independent study or two. These spaces allow for the kind of ongoing piloting we discuss in this example, where each separate piece of the research, conducted over a series of semesters, is actually a part of a whole. Because, as we have stated previously, action research is typically so time consuming, the piloting can get the process started earlier in one's graduate program.

Because many insider researchers come to their studies through puzzles in their own practices or sites, it is often difficult to discern the actual beginning of the research. It is not atypical to be informally problem solving or trying out various interventions in one's work site; action research moves this problem-solving process to a more formal level involving systematic data gathering and analysis. Because many doctoral students work full time, they bring to their doctoral studies real-life quandaries they are facing professionally; these professional puzzles often become the ones they then choose to pilot in their action research.

Unlike most work sites, universities divide coursework into semesters or quarters, increments of time that may not have much meaning in terms of a research cycle. The advantage of being able to extend an action research project over successive semesters is so the research does not have to be forced into, contained by, or truncated by the semester-long timeline. Rather, students can continue to document the cycles of inquiry across and beyond these arbitrary timelines. What this requires, though, is a professor or several willing to see this kind of piloting in an expansive way. Each course paper becomes a work in progress, part of a larger whole.

We offer the work of John Mark Dyke, a doctoral student working on his dissertation at the time of this writing, as an example of a work in progress. What eventually became the focus for his dissertation research began as a project in a practitioner research class, designed for students to do action research in their own sites. Fascinated with the possibilities of action research, Dyke continued his research the next semester through an independent study. Steeped in various research approaches, he eventually decided to build on his action research pilots for his dissertation research.

FIRST PHASE OF THE WORK

Working full time in Child Protective Services (CPS), Dyke's research evolved out of an issue in his workplace and guidelines put forth in federal policy. At issue was how many cases of substantiated child maltreatment came back into the system during a 12-month period. The federal standard for repeat maltreatment is 6.1, meaning CPS should have 6 or fewer resubstantiations out of 100 cases during a 12-month period.

> The Federal government can reduce funds to CPS agencies if they do not substantially meet this standard. The apparent intention of the Federal government in developing this standard is for CPS workers to intervene in abusive families' lives in such a way as to reduce the chance of these same families being re-referred to CPS for investigation and subsequently substantiated (Dyke, personal communication, 2002).

Many of us, in various fields, struggle with the implementation of guidelines and standards developed by outside, governing entities. In addition, these guidelines often contain injunctions to develop improvement plans to meet the standards imposed or face punitive damages of some sort. For example, many educators are currently struggling with the repercussions of the No Child Left Behind Act, federal legislation that may be used to put a school on probationary status; a school on probation is then required to initiate and implement an improvement plan. Action researchers seem particularly well poised to bring an authenticity to this planning and problem-solving process. Partly this is because the level of tacit knowledge brought into the process by professionals is kicked up a notch through the systematic inquiry that action research requires.

As I looked around the room, I noticed several of my fellow managers' heads were drooping. We have been in this meeting for six hours, listening to trainers tell us about Medicaid, managed care and budget cuts. What next? The head of the social services department moves to the front of the room. "Listen up people, this is important. It seems we are resubstantiating too many cases of child abuse and the Feds don't like it. The National Standard for recurrence of a substantiated child abuse allegation is 6.1%; our average is 8.1%. . . . If this keeps up, the Department could lose money, maybe not for several years, but you could lose money sooner. Starting now, if the resubstantiation number is too high you are not going to get a raise. And the Federal government is telling us that we have to come up with a per-formance improvement plan (PIP) to explain how we are going to lower the rate of reoccurrence of child abuse." The problem with this line of thinking was that I did not believe a substantiated allegation accurately equated to child maltreatment.

The Division Director's comments prompted me to question the reliability of the decision to substantiate or not substantiate an allegation. During my career, I spent four years investigating over 400 child abuse cases as a Protective Services' investigator and three more years supervising investigators. For each case I had to substantiate or unsubstaniate the allegation of maltreatment. The supervisor had to approve this decision, but it was pretty much left for me to decide. . . . My seven years involvement with investigating maltreatment led me to believe that the deci-sion to substantiate or unsubstantiate an allegation of child maltreatment was probably very unreliable.

After the meeting in which the head of the department announced the penalties of too many resubstantiations, I met with several of my colleagues. Together we expressed a great deal of interest in examining the decision to substantiate/unsubstantiate. This interest included a desire to improve the process, once we knew more about it. We decided that since I had the most train-ing in research design and data analysis (I was currently completing my degree work on a Ph.D.) I would put something together and present it at the next manager meeting. (Dyke, 2002, pp. 2–3).

To reiterate in terms of the above example: Many of us will face standards or guidelines imposed from the outside that possibly result in "improvement plans." These have the potential to be authentic plans that probe or ask, "What are the 'real' issues we are trying to solve here?" This moves issues beyond simple compliance to asking more authentic questions. In this example, there is own-ership of the "problem" beyond the researcher to a consensus among colleagues that the statistical evidence needs to be clarified—that is, what is it they are really trying to solve?

ITERATIVE CYCLES OF INQUIRY

The first round of data gathering focused on how workers thought through their rationale in substantiating or not substantiating cases of alleged abuse. Dyke's experience as a frontline worker informed his own sense that many factors figured into this equation. He listened carefully and took notes as social workers presented their cases. . . . Previous to beginning the study, I had asked investigative workers why they wanted to substantiate or unsubstantiated an allegation, but now I paid even more attention to their rationales. (Dyke, 2002, p. 3)

The question under study at this point was, "How reliable is the decision to substantiate/unsubstantiate an allegation of child maltreatment?" As someone who had faced the complexity of this decision himself, Dyke knew how multifaceted this decision was, and how any number of things impacted the decision-making process.

In order to answer this question, I designed an instrument with 9 investigative scenarios. . . . As a manager of a small CPS office, I supervised a secretary, a supervisor, and several investigative workers. Supervising investigative CPS workers provided me with an insider opportunity to gather information representative and relevant to the investigative decision. This information was not hypothetical but based on actual case staffings. (Dyke, 2002, pp. 4–5)

The devised instrument contained investigative scenarios that asked participants to rate the scenario along a four-point scale (definitely substantiate, probably substantiate, probably unsubstantiate, and definitely unsubstantiate). To try out the instrument, it was first presented to a wide range of protective service workers and then later presented to a group of CPS managers. Participants were asked to fill out the instrument, rating the scenarios as well as commenting on the scenarios. Piloting the instrument also allowed participants to discuss their rationales in rating the various scenarios. As is common in action research, just raising the research question and designing a way to study it is often already an intervention into the setting. In this case, workers were able to hash out together the complexity of the decision making and make explicit their own thinking. This became the model for the data collection: Participants would fill out the instrument, making their individual decisions regarding the scenarios, but, upon completion of this part, they would then discuss together the scenarios and their rationales for substantiating a case or not. Prior to the discussion, the aggregate results of the ratings were presented to each group so that the range of responses could be included in the discussion.

It seemed important to present the results immediately following the participants completing the instruments because we as an agency have experienced many researchers collecting information and never informing us of the results. In order to protect the privacy of participants, they were asked to fill out the instruments without including any identifying information. (Dyke, 2002, p. 6)

What they determined through this initial phase of data gathering was that there was substantial disagreement regarding the decision to substantiate or not substantiate allegations of child maltreatment in six of the nine cases presented in the scenarios. To further confirm these results, the instrument was more widely distributed and again the results suggested a lack of agreement on the substantiation decision. The initial concern that started this research was the possible repercussions of having a high rate of resubstantiations as indicted through the federal data. This round of data gathering indicated that determining whether to substantiate child maltreatment in the first place was no easy decision. Workers across the agency approached the decision differently and there was substantial disagreement as played out in the case scenarios.

As should be obvious by now, the action research initiated was generating a lot of fruitful discussion among agency workers. The beginning of data gathering was an intervention in itself. Interestingly, while Dyke was pursuing this research, he had simultaneously been conducting a pilot study on how teachers assign grades to children's writing. He had assumed that the decision making regarding how teachers assigned grades would be his "real" research; in fact, he successfully defended a dissertation proposal on this topic and was approved to proceed with it. His action research and his real research were running on parallel tracks, with the common denominator being a fascination with how workers/teachers arrive at decisions and determinations in ambiguous arenas. In the writing project research, he was an outsider documenting the process, whereas in the child maltreatment study, he was very much the insider initiating change.

THE DISSERTATION RESEARCH—A WORK IN PROGRESS

Having established that individual workers—frontline as well as supervisors—vary widely in their decision to substantiate or unsubstantiate the same case scenario, Dyke turned his attention to the small teams that have input into the custody decisions.

> The CPS worker routinely makes decisions with his/her supervisor, and may include others, such as a CPS attorney, a mid-level manager, a person from an external agency, and/or a family member in the decision-making process. The decisions made by this small group determines who has legal custody of the child, the living arrangements for the child, and the course of intervention necessary to assure the safety and well-being of the child. (Dyke, 2003, p. 2)

The focus for the dissertation study is on how CPS staff make the custody decision as a team.

> The primary research question is, How do Child Protective Services (CPS) make the custody decision with-one-another? More specifically this study will focus on the current status of how CPS staff actually make the custody decision with-one-another and how they would like to (ideally) make the decision together. (Dyke, 2003, pp. 4–5)

Participants in this part of the study include the players involved in the decision-making process for a case: the worker, supervisor, attorney, and manager.

As an experienced insider to CPS, Dyke knew that these decisions were not arrived at individually. Seeing the wide variance in decisions in the cases used in the pilot instrument, Dyke began to wonder how these various viewpoints come into play when the small team of folks involved in a custody case have to arrive at a decision together. His rationale, then, in proposing this part of the study is the following:

> It is assumed that the decision to remove or not remove a child from his/her care-taker is fraught with trauma for all persons involved. Furthermore, this decision is ill defined, the alternatives are endless, and the consequences of the decision are at best speculative. The decision occurs under stressful working conditions within the context of a bureaucracy. Knowledge gained through this study will support CPS staff in their effort to make the *best possible* decisions. (Dyke, 2003, pp. 5–6)

With an eye toward minimal disruption of the decision-making process, data collection will include surveys and semistructured interviews.

Over a period of 2 years, Dyke has been studying how the bureaucracy in which he works makes decisions about possible child maltreatment. He has included his coworkers in the inquiry and reflective process, with his data-gathering techniques already generating considerable discussion. His dissertation research is the next step in what he sees as collecting information on the decision-making process. While it is a "new" piece of research, it is very much nested in the work that he has done previously on this topic.

Conclusion

We have provided three very different dissertations that reflect very different research contexts, and yet all fit within action research's general tenets. Each of the approaches has advantages and disadvantages. Maguire (1993), after doing a PAR dissertation similar to McIntyre's, but with formerly battered women, cautions that PAR is extremely difficult to do alone and without funding.

> It may be easiest and most instructive to try becoming involved in an ongoing or established participatory research project, in which you can contribute your work without having to mobilize the entire project from scratch. You might consider trying to put together a team, even of other graduate students, to work in a con-text in which you're already established. Don't overlook the organizations, groups, or agencies in which you are already involved, regardless of how "reformist" you may initially assess them. You will inevitably make choices based on time constraints.

The dissertation should be an integral part of your life work, but don't let it expand to become a lifetime project. However, make no mistake, the entire participatory research process takes time. (p. 175)

Unlike Maguire, who had to track down participants and organize meetings with women who often had no transportation, McIntyre's student teachers were easily accessible and her project was intentionally time limited. Dyke's study is more open-ended because he is an employee in the site and his research meets goals of the bureaucracy for which he works as well as the requirements of his doctoral program. There are always trade-offs and compromises, but doctoral students seldom have the time or money to make the dissertation a lifetime project. It may be a piece of one's research agenda that continues for some time.

James Kelly, who led the PAR project that Lynne Mock worked with, has reflected on some of the problems associated with doing large-scale funded projects and involving graduate students in them. He says that were he to do the project over,

more attention would be given to creating a more supportive environment for community research at the university. For example, deadlines designed to move graduate students through the program as quickly as possible may need to be relaxed to provide the time required to build the necessary community relationships on which research can be developed. Also, the criteria for various program requirements such as theses and preliminary/comprehensive examinations could be designed to better-fit meaningful research in a community setting. Less focus on a specific curriculum of required courses and more opportunities for theoretical training based on a community research project could lessen the often-felt tensions between community and classroom demands. Establishing an advisory board of researchers and community leaders could facilitate problem solving. (Kelly et al., 2004, p. 216)

While very different in structure, tone, and context, what all of the studies described above have in common is that they produced knowledge that was not only fed back into the setting, but also contributed to a conversation taking place in a larger scientific and practitioner community. To use Cochran-Smith and Lytle's (1993) terminology, these studies produced both *local* and *public* knowledge.

In using very different examples of action research dissertations, we are hoping to give a sense of the possibilities as well as the strengths and challenges of the various approaches. Each researcher faces a complex set of issues in embarking on the research, whether it is resources, access, multiple roles, support, and so forth. This complexity carries into the next chapter, where we address ethical issues and gaining institutional approvals for action research.

7

Action Research, Ethics, and the Institutional Review Board

E thical issues enter into every phase of an action research dissertation, from the design to the actual execution of the proposal to the representation and dissemination of the data. In planning the research, doctoral students should do their best to anticipate the things their participants might face in the research process and work to minimize any risks that potentially come with being a participant. Because action research is a dynamic, evolving practice, there is no foolproof plan to avoid ethical dilemmas as the research develops. Cassell (1982) suggests that perhaps most important to the process is the ability to recognize an ethical issue when it arises so that it can be taken into consideration; the work, then, is not to anticipate every possible ethical conundrum as much as to commit to addressing them as they arise. Doctoral students should go into the field expecting to face ethical challenges.

When research involving human subjects is supported by federal funds or is under the auspices of institutions receiving federal support (most universities), an institutional review board (IRB) reviews the proposed research with an eye toward protecting the rights and welfare of "human subjects"[7] (Pritchard, 2002). Obviously, IRB approval is important in that the research can not move ahead without it, but action researchers must approach the approval process as the beginning point to an ongoing questioning of themselves and the construction of an ethical research process. We make the case that this is particularly important in light of the evolutionary nature of action research. It must be acknowledged that there will never be foolproof rules in place that cover all exigencies of research and, therefore, much is asked of action researchers in terms of continuously exercising professional judgment.

Background to the Creation of the IRB

Codes for conduct in research came out of atrocious abuses that came to light during the Nuremberg war crime trials at the end of World War II. When the biomedical experiments conducted by physicians and scientists on prisoners in concentration camps were exposed, there was a startling new awareness of the vulnerability of those held captive, who were subjected to experiments they never consented to, conducted by those in power or in positions of authority. The result was the Nuremberg Code, which "became the prototype of many later codes . . . intended to assure that research involving human subjects would be carried out in an ethical manner" (National Commission, 1979, p. 1).

In the U.S., several landmark cases of research that exploited particularly vulnerable populations laid the groundwork for the federal protections that were developed to minimize risk to human subjects participating in research (LeCompte & Schensul, 1999). These primarily involved abuses by the medical community that were publicly exposed in the mid-1960s and the early 1970s. Some of the more infamous cases included hepatitis vaccine research carried out on institutionalized, developmentally disabled children at the Willowbrook State School in New York and the Tuskegee Syphilis Study involving African American male prisoners from whom effective treatment for syphilis was withheld to track the progression of the disease (Mastroianni & Kahn, 2001). Mastroianni and Kahn point out that these examples of exploitive practices in research

> contributed to a sense that human subjects research in the US permitted scandalous practices—inadequate attempts to inform subjects about research and obtain their consent, exploitive recruitment strategies, the use of vulnerable subject populations, and a willingness to expose subjects to significant risk without any potential for direct medical benefit. Further, there was a sense that the risk and benefits of the research were split apart—the risks were borne by subjects, the benefits accrued to others. (p. 22)

This history of research abuses led to the creation of ethics policies focusing on the protection of human subjects from exploitation or exposure to unacceptable levels of risk through their participation in research. In addition, some populations, such as prisoners and children, were declared in need of special protections. Federal regulations to address these ethical concerns have their origins in the Belmont Report, issued by the National Commission for the Protection of Human Subjects of Biomedical and Behavioral Research in 1979. This report set out the basic ethical premises that are embodied in current regulations (Hammack, 1997) and are reflected both in professional associations' codes of ethics and in the establishment of IRBs. While created in an era of heightened awareness and concern about the ethics and abuses of biomedical research, the guidelines in the Belmont Report also apply to any field of research involving human subjects.

THE BELMONT REPORT

While the Belmont Report has been codified into working rules of sorts, implemented and enforced by entities such as IRBs, it is acknowledged in the report itself that it was intended as a guide rather than a clear-cut blueprint. The creators indicate that the rules "often are inadequate to cover complex situations; at times they come into conflict, and they are frequently difficult to interpret or apply" (National Commission, 1979, p. 3).

Three basic principles are set forth in the Belmont Report to provide an analytical framework toward the resolution of ethical problems that develop with research involving human subjects: (a) respect of persons, (b) beneficence, and (c) justice. The principles provide a framework within which to think about risks to human subjects participating in research; in addition, they "provide a basis on which specific rules may be formulated, criticized and interpreted" (National Commission, 1979, p. 3). Key here is that the principles offer an approach or guide rather than a grid that can be applied to resolve beyond dispute any ethical problem; with the ongoing development of action research, we must continue to push to understand the application of these principles to these emergent designs.

Respect for persons represents flip sides of the same idea: that individuals are autonomous persons, capable and entitled to personal decision making in terms of participating or not in the research process; conversely, if their autonomy is diminished, they are persons in need of protection in terms of their possible participation in the research process (National Commission, 1979, p. 4). Autonomous persons in this context are those who are seen as capable of deliberating and then acting upon this deliberation in terms of freely consenting or declining to participate in the proposed research. In other words, when approached, they freely consent or decline based on their weighing of the options and choices in front of them; part of this weighing is their consideration of whether they run the risk of being harmed in any way through or by the research and whether they are willing to assume such a risk.

In terms of respecting potential research participants, the researcher is obliged to be forthcoming in terms of imparting the information necessary whereby the potential participant can consent to participate based on being apprised of relevant information; part of the relevant information is a complete description of what the participant might expect if agreeing to be involved in the research. This has typically involved a spelling-out of the procedures of the research—observations, interviews, anything that the participant will be asked to do as part of the research. The idea is that the potential participant is fully informed as to what to expect in the research process. While this information may be conveyed verbally, it must also be laid out in written form; participants must agree in writing to the terms of the research via signing an informed consent form. Most IRBs supply a template of sorts that delineates what needs to be included in the consent form.

Some individuals are not seen as capable of self-determination—that is, able to give their own consent to participate in a research endeavor—and therefore are offered special protections based on their possible vulnerability (Tisdale, 2003). Diminished autonomy may be temporary, dependent on the maturation process of the individual or the life circumstances, or it may be permanent. For example, children are a population requiring special protection because they are seen as too young and immature to consent for themselves until they reach the age of 18. Others, such as the severely developmentally disabled or the mentally ill, no matter what age, may be seen as permanently not capable of self-determination and others—parents or guardians—may be asked to consent for them in terms of their participation in the research.

Those persons in life circumstances where they may be subtly coerced or unduly influenced to participate in the research, that is, perhaps not freely and voluntarily consenting, are also entitled to consideration regarding special protections. Prisoners are offered as a common example of those who may face coercion. In their circumstances, prisoners may fear some sort of repercussion should they refuse to participate or anticipate some kind of benefit should they agree; in either case, their ability to *freely* consent or decline may be compromised. These same concerns are often raised when teachers propose studying their own students or administrators their own employees. In these cases, the issue is one of deciding whether to allow them to "volunteer" at all or to "protect" them from even facing such a decision.

The principle of *justice* in research speaks to the fair distribution of the burdens and benefits of research in the selection and recruitment of participants (Mastroianni & Kahn, 2001; Pritchard, 2002). Mastroianni and Kahn (2001) point out that in practice this has also come to mean preventing any further exploitation of vulnerable groups; much was staked on protection and singling out particular groups (prisoners, children, pregnant women, and fetuses) for particular protections. The Belmont Report drew attention to the consideration of the preexisting vulnerability of potential participants based, in part, on past abuses. For example, prisoners were considered vulnerable because of their living environment and the constrained autonomy that came with it; in addition, they had been a population made easily available to researchers, in part because they, historically, had been viewed as less than "desirable" (Tisdale, 2003). Policies remain in place today that prevent research on prison populations unless there is a direct medical benefit to the individuals themselves, such as in clinical trials for HIV, or aims at better understanding or improving the prison environment such that the research would potentially benefit the prison population generally (Mastroianni & Kahn, 2001). Similarly, because of previous abuses such as the Willowbrook case mentioned previously, research involving children was limited to studies involving either minimal risk or direct medical benefits.

Some have argued that "deviant" people fit the category of vulnerable populations as defined by the Belmont Report. The reasoning is that deviant behavior is outside the accepted norm, and those exhibiting such behaviors fall into the undesirable category delineated in the report; O'Connor (1979, cited in Tisdale, 2003) suggests that illicit drug users and "sexual deviants" deserve special protections because they can be considered vulnerable if researchers place "further burdens on already burdened persons" (O'Connor, 1979, p. 18, cited in Tisdale, 2003, p. 21). The Belmont Report directs that researchers not select only "undesirable" persons for risky research (Tisdale, 2003). In addition, it stipulates that when selecting participants, care must be given to avoid systematically selecting those who are easily available (persons confined to institutions, welfare clients, etc.), easily manipulated, or in a compromised position; instead, the selection of subjects must directly relate to the research problem being studied. In addition, the principle of justice demands that, in the development of therapeutic devices, interventions, and procedures, these not advantage only those who can afford them and also that this kind of research not unduly involve persons from groups unlikely to benefit from the applications of the research.

The principle of *beneficence* speaks to the maximizing of benefits and the minimizing of risks in the research process. According to the Belmont Report, researchers are to adhere to two general rules: (a) do no harm and (b) maximize possible benefits and minimize possible harms (National Commission, 1979, p. 6). Essentially, "we must actively attempt not only to avoid harms, but to benefit those studied, to augment, not merely respect, their autonomy" (Cassell, 1982, p. 27).

However, as the report points out, to avoid harm requires learning what is harmful and, in the process of determining this, some may be exposed to risk of harm.

Learning what will, in fact, benefit may require exposing persons to risk. The problem posed by these imperatives is to decide when it is justifiable to seek certain benefits despite the risks involved, and when the benefits should be forgone because of the risks (National Commission, 1979, p. 7).

The principle of beneficence applies to individual research projects and the entire enterprise of research; by this we mean that researchers and IRBs must consider how to maximize benefits and reduce risks in the individual's research process, but this also must be done within the context of the longer-term benefits and risks that may result "from the improvement of knowledge and from the development of novel medical, psycho therapeutic, and social procedures" (National Commission, 1979, p. 7).

Researchers and the institutions designed to review research are asked to perform a balancing act; they are asked to take into consideration the possible risks and benefits of a course of research and make difficult decisions when the principle of beneficence cannot be unambiguously applied. Just as the Belmont Report reiterates an expectation that physicians are guided by the Hippocratic oath, requiring them to "do no harm," "according to their best judgment," this same sense of exercising professional judgment is required of us as action researchers.

The Role of the IRB

The paramount purpose of the IRB is to protect the rights and welfare of human subjects (McCarthy, 1998). The research activity only falls under the purview of the IRB if it involves human subjects; this means the researcher is proposing to obtain data from a living individual or through review of identifiable private information (Pritchard, 2002).

IRB approval is required if the research is funded by the U.S. government; this would include virtually all research carried out by those affiliated with a university because these institutions typically receive support from the federal government (LeCompte & Schensul, 1999). However, although all research should be submitted to the IRB, they generally exempt research that does not involve human subjects. Beyond the IRB approval, LeCompte & Schensul (1999) point out that all researchers are bound by professional ethics to protect the people they study from harm.

Drawing on the principles of the Belmont Report to guide them, IRBs are charged with the review of planned research with an eye toward protecting the rights and welfare of human subjects and ensuring the ethical treatment of possible participants; the IRB does this specifically through the evaluation of informed consent, the execution of a risk/benefit assessment, and the selection of potential participants for the research. Pritchard (2002, p. 8) outlines four different risk assessment functions of the IRB review: (a) what are the risks of the proposed research; (b) whether the risks have been minimized; (c) whether the risks constitute minimal risk; and (d) whether the risks are outweighed by the potential benefits and the importance of the knowledge that is expected to result from the research.

IRBS AND ACTION RESEARCH

While charged with applying federal guidelines, IRBs operate in specific, local contexts. It behooves any researcher to explore the local climate of the IRB and get a sense of how comfortable it is with action research. Conversations with academics and graduate students across institutions reveal wide variance in terms of working with the research approval process. This varies from a fairly smooth working relationship where action research proposals are seen as no more contested than any other, to those who report intense scrutiny, to delays in the approval process, and even to proposal denials. Some of this variance can be attributed to constructing *rules* out of the Belmont Report rather than continuing to explore how the principles apply and are honored as research approaches evolve; we continue this exploration below as we discuss specific aspects of the review process. Most university IRB websites provide a manual or guide to submitting the actual form for review. In most cases, the rationale behind the process, such as a copy of the Belmont Report, is included as well. Because these are typically fairly well spelled out in terms of the step-by-step expectations, we do not go into depth on these here; rather, we discuss how these expectations may or may not coincide with the realities of action research.

Issues With/of Informed Consent

To the degree that they are capable, research subjects should be given the opportunity to choose whether or not to participate in the research; toward this end, they must be given enough information to form this judgment (National Commission, 1979). Two central elements that the IRB considers in informed consent are the absence of coercive pressure to participate and the presentation of information regarding the research to inform the decision to participate (Tanke & Tanke, 1982). Typically, researchers are asked to initially describe the purposes of the research and the procedures to the potential participants; if they express interest in participating, potential participants are then given a consent form. The consent form is a clear spelling-out of what the participant can expect should he or she be involved in the research process. The IRB is concerned that the human subject's consent to participate is informed and voluntary, and that the participant is competent to give consent. What look like fairly straightforward procedures to judge informed consent get muddied with action research.

As we have made clear elsewhere in this book, the relationships between the researcher and the participants take multiple forms, depending on the researcher's positionality or location in terms of the research being undertaken, which can potentially blur the taken-for-granted assumptions of the researcher and the researched. Just as action research processes evolve over the course of the research, so do these relationships; for example, the starting point for the working relationship may be researcher and research participant, but may lead, over time, to coinvestigators. This kind of collaboration and coinvestigation can cross traditionally hierarchical lines such as that of a teacher and her pupils

(Anderson, Herr, & Nihlen, 1994), further muddying taken-for-granted assumptions as to who can be the researcher and who is the research participant.

These shifting relationships make it difficult to tack down who is consenting to what. The informed consent procedures also obscure the sense of agency that many participants have as they join the action research process. Because they are often part of the ongoing decision making regarding next steps in the research process, and because data collected are folded back into the very sites they occupy, participants often have a sense of coconstructing the processes of research rather than consenting to participate in something designed by others. Nevertheless, current procedures stipulate that prospective subjects be fully informed of what to expect in the research process; as Pritchard (2002) points out, these research processes are not fully formed a priori in action research, so the ability to fully inform potential participants is limited. The idea of coconstruction of research procedures is difficult to insert in conventions designed with other research paradigms in mind (Zeni, 2001).

In addition, researchers are required to apprise the IRB of any change in the research that may involve a shift in what was originally asked of the participants when the protocol was initially reviewed and approved; researchers often discover the changes are more in degree than drastic new measures that were not originally specifically included. But IRBs vary widely in their interpretations regarding what are significant enough changes whereby the researcher should consult them again for a revised approval and/or new consent forms for the participants. Some have asked action researchers to resubmit their plans with every new action research spiral as the researchers assess where the data and actions are now taking them in terms of the inquiry; most IRBs are comfortable with the ongoing evolution of action research once it has begun and give approval for the overall process.

The informed consent procedure does not adequately capture the dynamic nature of the evolving research procedures and relationships. The consent process as currently laid out through IRB procedures is a fairly static, one-time consent that poorly captures the possibility of the evolving research relationship and process. Tisdale (2003, citing Thorn, 1980) points out that informed consent has been critiqued as a meaningless ritual rather than something that addresses and improves the ethics of research that veers from that of experimental methods to more field based, or, we would add, action research.

Instead, action researchers are increasingly seeing the initial consent to participate in the research as the first of ongoing interactions around continued participation (Zeni, 2001). Standard consent forms clearly state that participants may voluntarily withdraw and cease participation in the research at any time and this, of course, applies to participants in action research as well. But beyond this, action researchers are suggesting that it behooves us to keep participants continually apprised as to how the research is evolving, and, if they are not involved in the research decision making, to explain what might be asked of them next. This idea of "processual consent" (Rosenblatt, 1995, cited in Tisdale, 2003, p. 26) is seen as a supplement to traditional informed consent; the goal in the case of action research is to repeatedly make clear the ongoing direction of the research itself (what further data may be asked from participants and what this will involve) as well as next steps that would be involved for participants. In addition, Smith (1990, cited in Zeni, 2001, p. 161) stresses the need for ongoing dialogue between the researcher and the participants, to move beyond what he terms as "contract" relationships toward "covenants" of trust. Howe and Moses (1999) note that some have "proposed construing informed consent on the model of an ongoing 'dialogue' and have suggested periodic reaffirmations of consent . . . as the procedural embodiment of this notion" (p. 42).

In the same vein, Wax (1982) suggests that the relationships between researcher and participants should be models of "parity" and "reciprocity"; "where there is parity and reciprocity, the ethical quality of the relationship has progressed far beyond the requirements of 'informed consent'" (p. 46). Meason and Sikes (1992, cited in Ebbs, 1996) suggest that a more reciprocal interaction establishes a principle of respect where all concerned have a sense of the "rules, expectancies, understandings of the nature of a researcher/ researched relationship and a sense that both sides agree on the fairness of the bargain" (p. 4). This principle of respect and reciprocity addresses the idea that research participants must not be treated as a means toward an end, but rather as "reflective moral agents" who deserve to be treated with dignity (Pritchard, 2002).

The issue of subtle coercion or unduly influencing possible participants in terms of them freely or voluntarily consenting to participate in the research often arises in action research. This particularly comes into play when the researcher is an insider and is in a position of power in relationship to the potential participants, although outsiders often negotiate entry with gatekeepers, placing them in similar positions of power vis-à-vis participants. Examples of this include teachers and their students or administrators and their employees. The researcher's status as an authority may impinge on the voluntary nature of freely consenting, with subordinates fearing some kind of repercussion should they not "volunteer." Or, it may appear that the researcher has a "captive audience" of sorts, bringing with it another wrinkle in the research approval process. As Pritchard (2002) points out, just because practitioners are interested in research in their own sites, they do not have the right to "demand the cooperation of others" or the right "to compel people—including their students— to cooperate in their research" (p. 5). In the case of children, because of their protected status in the eyes of federal guidelines, it may be a matter of whether the research possibilities should even be broached to them and their parents. In essence, the question becomes one of whether the IRB thinks they should be given the possibility of participating in the research based on their assumption that the issue of coercion is inescapable in such a situation and, hence, jeopardizes voluntary consent.

Fear of the consequences of not participating or any other constraints surrounding the decision to participate in the research must be removed so the decision regarding participation is freely made (Hammack, 1997). Tanke and Tanke (1982) have suggested that those persons who are in roles to influence potential research participants, for example, classroom teachers or treating physicians, should avoid being the primary persons who seeks the subject's consent; they suggest this as a precaution to "divorce research from treatment or education in the subject's mind" (p. 136). In addition to this approach, it may also be possible for researchers to bring potential participants into the formative stages of the consent process. We are suggesting that it could be within keeping of the stance of action research to ask potential participants what kinds of conditions could be created that would allow them to freely consent to the research; for example, how would they suggest handling the worry that there could be reprisals for not participating? What could be put in place that would address this, from their point of view? We are suggesting that this is in keeping with the National Commission's (1979) idea of a standard of "the reasonable volunteer," one where the participant knows that the research is not such that it is necessary for their care or their benefit, but they "can decide whether they wish to participate in the furthering of knowledge" (p. 10).

Action research is, in part, about forging new types of research relationships; our sense is that this could extend to the consent process as well. It could even be seen as an advantage if, from the beginning of a potential research relationship, the participants are consulted regarding how to alleviate a sense of coercion. This immediately shifts the working relationship from one of the "expert" researcher informing the "subjects"—figuring out what is best for them without their input—to one of seeing if a collaborative research relationship can begin to be established. The "requirement that informed consent be obtained is derived primarily from the principle of respect for persons" (National Commission, 1979, p. 13), the spirit of which, we are suggesting, could be well served in this kind of collaborative construction of the consent process. Of course, in this kind of stance, the action researcher must be prepared to not move forward with the research if those concerned cannot together conceive of measures that could be put in place for them to feel safe or feel free enough not to consent.

Assessment of Risks and Benefits of the Research

The justification of research on the basis of a favorable risk/benefit assessment is drawn from the principle of beneficence; "the principle of beneficence actually reminds researchers of what it means to protect and do good" (Tisdale,

2003, p. 22). The research is, ideally, to do no harm and to maximize possible benefits and minimize possible harms (National Commission, 1979). All researchers are ethically bound to protect participants from treatment that would be harmful to them, whether physical, financial, emotional, or to their reputations (LeCompte & Schensul, 1999). Usual risks include possible embarrassment, invasion of privacy, or a breach of confidentiality (Tanke & Tanke, 1982). Federal rules require an assessment of all risks against benefits that may be produced; researchers are expected to make explicit who and/or what will benefit from the research (Hammack, 1997). The benefits are expected to outweigh the risks. Participants should clearly "understand the short- and long-term risks and volunteer to incur them" (LeCompte & Schensul, 1999, p. 183).

For the investigator, the assessment is a means to examine whether the proposed research is properly designed. For a review committee, it is a method for determining whether the risks that will be presented to subjects are justified. For prospective subjects, the assessment will assist the determination whether or not to participate (National Commission, 1979, p. 12).

As we pointed out earlier, it is not possible to know with certainty beforehand the risks that might be involved for research participants; this is thought to be particularly true in the case of action research, where the intent is to initiate a change process. The researcher's job is to use professional judgment in anticipating and minimizing risks that might occur to the participants. Tisdale (2003) points out that as researchers, we could never plan for all the possibilities that might occur, yet at the same time, we are responsible for all the possibilities. The IRB approval process is just the beginning of an ongoing assessment on the part of the researcher, whose responsibility is always to proceed with the best interests of participants in mind.

Because of the evolutionary nature of action research, IRBs are often wary of approving a process the course of which is yet to be determined (Hoonaard, 2001). In addition, the purposes of action research are fundamentally different from those of researchers committed to not disturbing or influencing research contexts; action researchers are committed to working toward change, whether in their own practices and contexts or in those into which they have been invited. We would, though, agree with Deyhle, Hess, and LeCompte (1992) that even outside of the action research paradigm, researchers must acknowledge the effects of their presence on the community being studied; otherwise, they are "not aware of the realities of the drama unfolding" around them (p. 622).

Codes of ethics and federal regulations are attempts to make explicit the commitment of researchers to the welfare of the research participants but these are, as Hammack (1997) points out, general specifications; this is to allow for professional judgment and authority when faced with problematic circumstances in the research endeavor. This stance is particularly important when considering that most of the suggested methods for minimizing risks and protecting human subjects are of little use in action research. Ethical safeguards for quantitative experimental research such as random selection, control groups, and removing of the personal influence of the researcher are, as Zeni (2001) observes, either irrelevant or problematic. In addition, traditional qualitative safeguards such as disguising the setting, using pseudonyms, or having anonymous informants may be difficult or not that relevant when data collected in the site are folded back into it for purposes of fostering change. As the data are brought back into the community, there is a worry that informants will be recognized or identifiable to the larger community (Pritchard, 2002); this kind of concern is then figured into the equation when IRBs calculate levels of risk. We suggest that the conventions for minimizing risk that are parts of other types of research are not very helpful for the action researcher and that IRBs expecting to see these in proposals are imposing fairly meaningless rituals on action researchers without providing much in the way of helpful guidance.

Close working relationships between the researcher and the participants as they collaborate make it fairly nonsensical that others local to the site would not know who are involved in the research. But we would also add that one of the points of action research is the realignment of the researcher/researched relationship that comes from doing research *with* rather than *on*. Within a more collaborative research stance, decision making is more of a shared process and insiders are part of the process in terms of assessing their own vulnerability as well as how to best return the data to the setting. Others (Ebbs, 1996; Wolf, 1996, cited in Knight, 2000) term it "empowering" when those who have traditionally been thought of as research subjects become involved in a more participatory model of research; data are continuously returned to them for appraisal, and decisions regarding its dissemination and use are jointly negotiated. Ironically, then, where some see risk, others see the very process of bringing the data back into the community from which it was generated as a benefit both for the researched and the community.

Lincoln (1993, cited in Ebbs, 1996) makes the case that through joint decision making about data collection, analysis, and writing, the researched will become empowered and will be the agents and instruments of their own change processes. Part of this sense of empowerment, Lincoln argues, is that the researched can come to terms with historical, social, and cultural contexts of their communities and their position in those contexts through the collaborative nature of the research. In this collaboration, the researcher can assume

an activist stance, forgo the "disinterested observer" role demanded by traditional research, and undertake consciousness-raising activities (community seminars, community-building activities, public meetings, group research design work, and the like) which enable the silenced to come to terms with their own historicity and personal locations. (1993, p. 43, cited in Ebbs, 1996, p. 3)

As we think, then, about possible risks to participants and assessing them in proposed research, we are reminded that participants are not to be treated as objects or means to an end; rather, they are to be treated with dignity and seen as reflective moral agents (Pritchard, 2002). Some would argue

> that past research paradigms of, for example, forced choice surveys, continue to silence voice and support a notion of managerialism and prescription. Casey claims that an instrumental view of the researched exists in which they are treated as objects which can be controlled and manipulated for the sake of the research. (Ebbs, 1996, p. 3, citing Casey, 1992)

Of course, a similar concern can be raised with action research if researchers have predetermined goals for those studied (Cassell, 1982) and are unwilling to interrogate their own, perhaps well-meaning, stance toward the community. We would suggest that one of the greatest safeguards to this is the reciprocal relationship stance discussed earlier where both the researcher and researched enter as colearners and coinvestigators. In these relationships, the researcher works closely with those studied to help determine the relevant problems, methods, and goals and how to achieve them. This stance, Cassell (1982) suggests, enhances "the autonomy of those studied, thereby treating people more fully as ends. Thus we might consider such research a paradigm of the ideal relationship between investigators and investigated" (p. 20).

In discussing more reciprocal research relationships, Wax (1982) makes the case that the researcher and the researched "recognize each other as fellow, moral human beings, and enforce on each other the adherence to a suitable set of moral norms" (p. 45). We suggest, then, that the researcher and the researched are in a relationship with each other where they hold each other to an ethical stance and way of being together that is coconstructed rather than externally regulated. May (1980, cited in Deyhle, Hess, & LeCompte, 1992) suggests that for the researcher, a positive contribution to the well-being of those researched takes precedence over any other obligations. It seems to us that this last injunction is very much in keeping with the principle of beneficence, which asks researchers to do no harm and to do good.

THE CHARGE FOR IRBs

A primary concern of would-be action researchers is that their proposals are reviewed using guidelines and questions designed with traditional scientific experiments in mind (Zeni, 2001) rather than action research. As Zeni points out, this mismatch between the guidelines and the realities of action research has left any number of researchers bewildered by the advice and research ethics dispensed from these structures designed for the protection of human subjects. This mismatch mirrors a previous struggle on the part of qualitative researchers when this form of research was initially gaining ground and struggling to gain credibility (Howe & Moses, 1999). Some qualitative researchers charged IRBs with being obstructive or hostile to their research (Murphy & Johannson, 1990, cited in Howe & Moses, 1999) or, at the very least, that their research approach was misunderstood.

Wax (1982) has argued that the analysis of ethical problems generated by varying forms of research "has been impoverished because of the insistence on regarding all research as if structured about the model of experimenter-subject" (p. 33). He goes on to make the case that in seeking to simplify ethical issues of research into universalistic formulations, bureaucrats have muddied the conversation in ways that are not of much help to researchers outside of this mold.

> When the experimenter-subject dyad is regarded as paradigmatic and normative, then ethical analysis becomes impoverished and those who wish to conduct ethically responsible research find themselves without guidance, while being themselves subjected to a regulatory process that may inflict a moral wrong on them. (Wax, 1982, pp. 33–34)

The federal regulations require that the IRB possess sufficient expertise to judge the research proposals it reviews (Hoonaard, 2001; Pritchard, 2002). Although it is important that IRBs develop an understanding of the risks and pressures peculiar to specific populations, others with specific expertise may be brought in as consultants at the request of either the committee or the researcher (Pritchard, 2002). Researchers may submit the names of individuals specifically qualified to review their proposals to the IRB for consideration. But IRBs that review a significant number of action research proposals should bring in as members those who are familiar with this approach to research (Pritchard, 2002); given the growing popularity of the approach, it is difficult to imagine an IRB that would not routinely want this expertise among its regular members.

Beyond this, if the IRB routinely reviews research involving specific populations or methodologies, it should develop guidelines to resolve recurrent questions (Tanke & Tanke, 1982). Tanke and Tanke suggest that if an issue continually arises, the IRB should work to resolve the issue and publish its policy decisions. We suggest that this kind of transparency in its dealings could serve an educative function for the research community over which the IRB has power but, in addition, it could open the IRB to scrutiny and perhaps challenge.

Many suggest that the ethical guidelines need to be rethought for action research (Zeni, 2001); the question is one of whether it is appropriate to judge the ethical merits of an approach such as action research using criteria derived from other paradigms of research (Hoonaard, 2001). A standoff of sorts is currently taking place where many action researchers see IRBs as gatekeepers or as a hindrance to their research or, worse, irrelevant. Action researchers can play a part in educating the IRB to the complexities of action research; while reporting our findings, we can also report our thinking through of the ethical situations we encounter in the field. This kind of information could be used to assist in a reading of the federal guidelines in light of the evolution and development of action research.

8

Final Thoughts

The action research dissertation is not for everyone. For those who have a low tolerance for ambiguity and messiness, action research would probably be best as the path not taken. But we have also seen doctoral students get "hooked" on the process of action research. Often, in initial pilot studies, they become clear that this is the type of research they want to pursue. We suggest to any doctoral student a "trying on" of the methodology, a toe in the water, prior to a firm commitment for the dissertation. Signing on as a research assistant in a larger action research study or through a smaller piloting in one's own area can serve this purpose.

We ourselves have been captivated working on our own action research projects. We have seen our professional practices evolve in relation to our learning in our own work sites through action research. It sustains us and nurtures us as professionals and can seemingly do so on an ongoing basis. Having said that, we remind doctoral students that although they very well may continue to carry out action research in their professional lives, the work they are doing for a dissertation is not a lifelong process. As we often tell our own doctoral students, "It's only a dissertation," as distinguished from a student's life work. Because of the evolving complexity of action research and a commitment to the change process, action research dissertations are time-consuming endeavors. In this sense, then, it behooves students, with their dissertation committees, to continue to discuss both how to commit to an action research process that has integrity while also bounding the process. This may be different than playing things out to the natural end of the research process and its multiple iterative cycles.

One caveat we offer here regarding the final write-up of the action research dissertation is that it does not automatically mean that there was a "successful" change effort to document with a happy ending—although it might. Rather, our goal as researchers is the documentation of working to understand and initiate change in the contexts being studied. Part of this documentation could include how the change process was obstructed or not seen as viable despite persistent efforts. These "failed" attempts are important to document in terms of increasing our understanding of the complexity of the change process. This complexity has been elegantly described by Hans van Beinum (1999):

> One of the things one learns is that there is no relationship between the way a problem has structured itself and presents and the logic of a discipline. One has to "move" (figuratively speaking) from within the field. One of the classical mistakes one can make is to come too quickly with the right interpretation. One has to fight one's tendency to reduce the Other to the Same, to reduce the situation to one's theory. To struggle with the notion and the practice that ethics comes before epistemology. . . . One moves from practice to practice, and perhaps from practice to "theory." In action research one starts in the middle and ends in the middle. (p. 19)

Action research has often been thought of as a process that produces local knowledge. With more doctoral students using it for their dissertations, it also clearly has the potential to inform the knowledge bases of our fields of study. We encourage doctoral students to move their work beyond their dissertations into the realms of publishing. By going public with our work, we learn from and inform each other, pushing our respective fields of study as well as the methodology itself. By doing this, we come full circle: In the documenting of the change effort, academe too is potentially challenged to encompass methodological progressions and breakthroughs.

Appendix

KEY RESOURCES FOR DOCTORAL
STUDENTS DOING ACTION RESEARCH DISSERTATIONS

The following sources provide a sufficiently sophisticated approach to action research for a doctoral dissertation. It is easy to become overwhelmed when starting out. Begin with a good overview and then read in the specific area you are interested in. If you are an insider to the setting, start with Cochran-Smith and Lytle's (1993) *Inside/Outside: Teacher Research and Knowledge.* If you are an outsider to the setting, start with Greenwood and Levin's (1998) *Introduction to Action Research: Social Research for Social Change.* Both of these books are highly intelligent introductions to the methodology, although written from their own particular perspectives. Reason and Bradbury's (2001) *Handbook of Action Research: Participative Inquiry and Practice* provides an extensive overview of the various paradigms and perspectives available to action researchers. See Dick (1993) for an excellent and useful resource geared directly to the preparation of an action research thesis or dissertation.

Anderson, G. L. (2002). Reflecting on research for doctoral students in education. *Educational Researcher, 31*(7), 22–25.

Anderson, G. L., & Herr, K. (1999). The new paradigm wars: Is there room for rigorous practitioner knowledge in schools and universities? *Educational Researcher, 28*(5), 12–21.

Anderson, G. L., Herr, K., & Nihlen, A. (1994). *Studying your own school: An educator's guide to qualitative practitioner research.* Thousand Oaks, CA: Sage.

Argyris, C., Putnam, R., & Smith, D. M. (1985). *Action science: Concepts, methods, and skills for research and intervention.* San Francisco: Jossey-Bass.

Brooks, A., & Watkins, K. (1994). A framework for using action technologies. In A. Brooks and K. Watkins (Eds.), *The emerging power of action technologies* (pp. 99–111). San Francisco: Jossey-Bass.

Bullough, R. V., & Pinnegar, S. (2001). Guidelines for quality in autobiographical forms of self-study research. *Educational Researcher, 30*(3), 13–22.

Cochran-Smith, M., & Lytle, S. (1993). *Inside/Outside: Teacher research and knowledge.* New York: Teachers College Press.

Carr, W., & Kemmis, S. (1986). *Becoming critical.* London: Falmer Press.

Connelly, F. M., & Clandinin, J. (1990). Stories of experience and narrative inquiry. *Educational Researcher, 19*(5), 2–14.

Dick, B. (1993). *You want to do an action research thesis? How to conduct and report action research.* Retrieved August 2003 from www.scu.edu.au/schools/gcm/ar/arthesis.html

Greenwood, D. (Ed.). (1999). *Action research: From practice to writing in an international action research development program.* Amsterdam: John Benjamins.

Greenwood, D., & Levin, M. (1998). *Introduction to action research: Social research for social change.* Thousand Oaks, CA: Sage.

Herr, K. (1995). Action research as empowering practice. *Journal of Progressive Human Services, 6*(2), 45–58.

Heron, J. (1996). *Co-operative inquiry: Research into the human condition.* London: Sage.

Maguire, P. (1987). *Doing participatory research: A feminist approach.* Amherst: The Center for International Education, University of Massachusetts.

Maguire, P. (1993). Challenges, contradictions, and celebrations: Attempting participatory research as a doctoral student. In P. Park, M. Brydon-Miller, B. Hall, & T. Jackson (Eds.), *Voices of change: Participatory research in the United States and Canada* (pp. 157–176). Westport, CT: Bergin & Garvey.

McTaggart, R. (Ed.). (1997). Participatory action research: International contexts and consequences. Albany, NY: SUNY Press.

Minkler, M., & Wallerstein, N. (Eds.). (2003). *Community-based participatory research for health.* San Francisco: Jossey-Bass.

Perry, C. (1998). *A structured approach to presenting theses: Notes for students and their supervisors.* Retrieved August 2003 from www.scu.edu.ar/schools/gcm/ar/art/cperry.html (A useful public domain resource, but not specifically focused on action research.)

Reason, P., & Bradbury, H. (Eds.). (2001). *Handbook of action research: Participative inquiry and practice* (pp. 81–90). Thousand Oaks, CA: Sage.

Schon, D. (1995). The new scholarship requires a new epistemology. *Change: The Magazine of Higher Learning, 27*(6), 27–34.

Tolman, D., & Brydon-Miller, M. (Eds.). (2001). *From subjects to subjectivities: A handbook of interpretive and participatory methods.* New York: New York University Press.

Notes

1. Because action research has not enjoyed legitimacy in the academy, many students and dissertation committees have not used the term *action research* for studies that are, in fact, action research. We have found that merely doing a search of *action research* or related terms may not be sufficient to locate many action research studies. Research-oriented Listservs are often another source for identifying action research studies on a particular topic.

2. The *Dialogues on Work and Innovation* series is edited by Hans van Beinum, Richard Ennals, Werner Fricke, and Oyvind Palshaugen. The *Practitioner Research* series is edited by Marilyn Cochran-Smith and Susan Lytle.

3. See Nancy Fraser's (1997) feminist critique of Habermas on this point. In this regard, it is important to point out that the researchers associated with this movement are largely male.

4. See Anderson and Grinberg (1998) and Barker (1993) for a poststructuralist discussion of how such groups can exercise what Barker calls *concertive control,* resulting in a more subtle, but effective, form of control.

5. Bray, Lee, Smith, and Yorks (2000) provide another approach to doing collaborative research while carving out individual dimensions of the research.

6. In these studies, the participants were volunteers who agreed to participate in the study. However, some practitioners choose to do PAR with their own students, clients, or patients. As we discussed in chapter 3, these issues of positionality have implications for the trustworthiness of the study and ethical implications that IRBs may have issues with.

7. Since the Nuremberg Code and the Belmont Report use the term *human subjects,* that is the language we will also use. A term such as *participant* may more accurately describe the research relationship where the research is often done *with* rather than *of* or *on subjects.*

References

Altricher, H., & Posch, P. (1989). Does the grounded theory approach offer a guiding paradigm for teacher research? *Cambridge Journal of Education, 19*(1).

Anderson, G. L. (1989). Critical ethnography in education: Origins, current status, and new directions. *Review of Educational Research, 59*(3), 249–270.

Anderson, G. L. (1999). Toward authentic participation: Deconstructing the discourse of participatory reforms. *American Educational Research Journal, 35*(4), 571–606.

Anderson, G. L. (2002). Reflecting on research for doctoral students in education. *Educational Researcher, 31*(7), 22–25.

Anderson, G. L., & Grinberg, J. (1998). Educational administration as a disciplinary practice: Appropriating Foucault's view of power, discourse, and method. *Educational Administration Quarterly, 34*(3), 329–353.

Anderson, G. L., & Herr, K. (1999). The new paradigm wars: Is there room for rigorous practitioner knowledge in schools and universities? *Educational Researcher, 28*(5), 12–21.

Anderson, G. L., Herr, K., & Nihlen, A. (1994). *Studying your own school: An educator's guide to qualitative practitioner research.* Thousand Oaks, CA: Sage.

Anderson, G. L., & Jones, F. (2000). Knowledge generation in educational administration from the inside-out: The promise and perils of site-based, administrator research. *Educational Administration Quarterly, 36*(3), 428–464.

Anzaldua, G. (1987). *Borderlands/La frontera: The new meztiza.* San Francisco: Aunt Lute.

Argyris, C., Putnam, R., & Smith, D. M. (1985). *Action science: Concepts, methods, and skills for research and intervention.* San Francisco: Jossey-Bass.

Argyris, C., & Schon, D. (1974). *Theory in practice: Increasing professional effectiveness.* San Francisco: Jossey-Bass.

Argyris, C., & Schon, D. (1991). Participatory action research and action science compared: A commentary. In W. F. Whyte (Ed.), *Participatory action research* (pp. 85–96). Newbury Park: Sage.

Asten, M. (1993). A study of lesbian family relationships: An interrelated filmed/ written ethnographic and feminist participatory study of lesbian families in American society (Doctoral dissertation. University of Cincinnati, 1993). *Dissertation Abstracts International, 55,* 232.

Atwell, N. (1982). Classroom-based writing research: Teachers learn from students. *English Journal, 71,* 84–87.

Ballenger, C. (1992). Because you like us: The language of control. *Harvard Educational Review, 62*(2), 199–208.

Ballenger, C. (1998). *Teaching other people's children: Literacy and learning in a bilingual classroom.* New York: Teachers College Press.

Barker, J. (1993). Tightening the iron cage: Concertive control in self-managing teams. *Administrative Science Quarterly, 38*(3), 408–437.

Barone, T. (2000). *Aesthetics, politics, and educational inquiry: Essays and examples.* New York: Peter Lang.

Bartunek, J., & Louis, M. R. (1996). *Insider/outsider team research.* Thousand Oaks, CA: Sage.

Battaglia, C. (1995). Confused on a higher level about more important things! In S. Noffke & R. Stevenson (Eds.), *Educational action research: Becoming practically critical* (pp. 74–91). New York: Teachers College Press.

Bell, E. L. (2001). Infusing race into the U.S. discourse on action research. In P. Reason & H. Bradbury (Eds.), *Handbook of action research: Participative inquiry & practice* (pp. 48–58). London: Sage.

Berger, P., & Luckmann, T. (1967). *The social construction of reality.* New York: Anchor Books.

Bissex, G., & Bullock, R. (1987). *Seeing for ourselves: Case study research by teachers of writing.* Portsmouth, NH: Heinemann.

Bochner, A., & Ellis, C. (2002). *Ethnographically speaking: Autoethnography, literature, and aesthetics.* Walnut Creek, CA: Altamira Press.

Bone, D. (1996). Quality management is collegiate management: Improving practice in a special school. In P. Lomax (Ed.), *Quality management in education: Sustaining the vision through action research* (pp. 152–165). London: Routledge.

Bradbury, H., & Reason, P. (2001). Conclusion: Broadening the bandwidth of validity: Issues and choice-points for improving the quality of action research. In P. Reason & H. Bradbury (Eds.), *Handbook of action research: Participative inquiry & practice* (pp. 447–455). London: Sage.

Bray, J., Lee, J., Smith, L., & Yorks, L. (2000). *Collaborative inquiry in practice: Action, reflection, and making meaning.* Thousand Oaks, CA: Sage.

Bronfenbrenner, U. (1979). *The ecology of human development.* Cambridge, MA: Harvard University Press.

Brookline Teacher Research Seminar. (2003). *Regarding children's words: Teacher research on language and literacy.* New York: Teachers College Press.

Brooks, A., & Watkins, K. E. (Eds.). (1994). *The emerging power of action inquiry technologies.* San Francisco: Jossey-Bass.

Brown, L. D., & Tandon, R. (1983). Ideology and political inquiry: Action research and participatory research. *The Journal of Applied Behavioral Science, 19*(3), 277–294.

Brown, P. A. (1993). Young mothers' voices: Reflections on abusive relationships, a feminist participatory research (Doctoral dissertation, University of San Francisco, 1993). *Dissertation Abstracts International, 55,* 490.

Bullough, R. V., & Pinnegar, S. (2001). Guidelines for quality in autobiographical forms of self-study research. *Educational Researcher, 30*(3), 13–22.

Carey, A. (1997). *Taking the risk out of democracy: Corporate propoganda versus freedom and liberty.* Urbana: University of Illinois Press.

Carr, W. (1989). Action research: Ten years on. *Journal of Curriculum Studies, 21,* 85–90.

Carr, W., & Kemmis, S. (1986). *Becoming critical.* London: Falmer Press.

Campbell, D. T., & Stanley, J. C. (1963). *Experimental and quasi-experimental designs for research.* Dallas: Houghton Mifflin.

Carter, K. (1993). The place of story in the study of teaching and teacher education. *Educational Researcher, 22*(1), 5–12.

Cassell, J. (1982). Harms, benefits, wrongs and rights in fieldwork. In J. E. Sieber (Ed.), *The ethics of social research: Fieldwork, regulation and publication* (pp. 49–70). New York: Springer-Verlag.

Chambers, R. (1994). The origins and practice of participatory rural appraisal. *World Development, 22*(7), 953–966.

Chambers, R. (1997). *Whose reality counts? Putting the first last.* London: Intermediate Technology Publications.

Chavez, V., Duran, B., Baker, Q., Avila, M., & Wallerstein, N. (2003). The dance of race and privilege in community based participatory research. In M. Minkler & N. Wallerstein (Eds.), *Community-based participatory research for health* (pp. 81–97). San Francisco: Jossey-Bass.

Chavis, D., Stucky, P., & Wandersman, A. (1983). Returning research to the community: A relationship between scientists and citizen. *American Psychologist 38,* 424–434.

Chisholm, L. (1990). Action research: Some methodological and political considerations. *British Educational Research Journal, 16*(3), 249–257.

Christman, J., Hirshman, J., Holtz, A., Perry, H., Spelkoman, R., & Williams, M. (1995). Doing Eve's work: Women principals write about their practice. *Anthropology and Education Quarterly, 26*(2), 213–227.

Clandinin, J., & Connelly, M. (1995). *Teachers' professional knowledge landscapes.* New York: Teachers College Press.

Clift, R., Veal, M. L., Holland, P., Johnson, M., & McCarthy, J. (1995). *Collaborative leadership and shared decision-making: Teachers, principals, and university professors.* New York: Teachers College Press.

Cochran-Smith, M., & Lytle, S. (1993). *Inside/Outside: Teacher research and knowledge.* New York: Teachers College Press.

Cochran-Smith, M., & Lytle, S. (1998). Teacher research: The question that persists. *International Journal of Leadership in Education, 1*(1), 19–36.

Collins, P. H. (1990). *Black feminist thought: Knowledge, consciousness and the politics of empowerment.* New York: Routledge.

Connelly, F. M., & Clandinin, J. (1990). Stories of experience and narrative inquiry. *Educational Researcher, 19*(5), 2–14.

Corey, S. M. (1949). Action research, fundamental research, and educational practices. *Teachers College Record, 50,* 509–514.

Corey, S. M. (1953). *Action research to improve school practices.* New York: Teachers College Press.

Corey, S. M. (1954). Action research in education. *Journal of Educational Research, 47,* 375–380.

Cornwall, A. (1996). Towards participatory practice: Participatory rural appraisal (PRA) and the participatory process. In K. De Koning & M. Martin (Eds.), *Participatory research in health: Issues and experience* (pp. 94–107). London: Zed Books.

Cunningham, J. B. (1983). Gathering data in a changing organization. *Human Relations, 36*(5), 403–420.

Delong, J. (2002). How can I improve my practice as a superintendent of schools and create my own living educational theory? (Doctoral dissertation, University of Bath, 2002). Retrieved February 12, 2004 from www.bath.ac.uk/~edsajw/living.shtml

de Schutter, A., & Yopo, B. (1981). *Investigacion participativa: Una opcion metodologica para la education de adultos* [Participatory research: A methodological option for adult education]. Patzcuaro, Michoacan: CREFAL.

Deyhle, D., Hess, G. A., Jr., & LeCompte, M. (1992). Approaching ethical issues for qualitative researchers in education. In M. LeCompte, W. Millroy, & J. Preissle

(Eds.), *The handbook of qualitative research in education* (pp. 597–641). San Diego, CA: Academic Press.

Dick, B. (2000) *Postgraduate programs using action research.* Retrieved February 2, 2004 from www.scu.edu.au/schools/gcm/ar/arp/ppar.html

Dickson, G. (1997). Participatory action research and health promotion: The grandmothers' story (Doctoral dissertation, University of Saskatchewan, 1997). *Dissertation Abstracts International, 64,* 1943.

Dickson, G., & Green, K. (2001). The external researcher in participatory action research. *Educational Action Research, 9*(2), 243–260.

Dockendorf, M. (1995). Within the labyrinth: Facilitating teacher research groups. (Master's thesis, Simon Fraser University, 1995). *Dissertation Abstracts International, 34,* 1333.

Dyke, J. M. (2002). *The substantiation decision within a protective services agency: A practitioner research approach.* Paper submitted to complete the requirement of an independent study.

Dyke, J. M. (2003). *An examination of how child protective staff make decisions with-one-another.* Dissertation proposal. University of New Mexico.

Ebbs, C. (1996). Qualitative research inquiry: Issues of power and ethics. *Education, 117,* 217–222.

Eisner, E. (1997). The promise and perils of alternative forms of data representation. *Educational Review, 26,* 4–10.

Elliott, J. (1991). *Action research for educational change.* Milton Keynes, UK: Open University Press.

Ellsworth, E. (1989). Why doesn't this feel empowering? Working through the repressive myths of critical pedagogy. *Harvard Educational Review, 59*(3), 297–324.

Engelstad, P. H., & Gustavsen, B. (1993). Swedish network development for implementing national work reform strategy. *Human Relations, 46*(2), 219–248.

Evans, M. (1995). An action research enquiry into reflection in action as part of my role as a deputy head teacher (Doctoral dissertation, University of Kingston, U.K.). Retrieved October 20, 2003 from www.bath.ac.uk/~edsajw/

Fals Borda, O. (2001). Participatory (action) research in social theory: Origins and challenges. In P. Reason & H. Bradbury (Eds.), *Handbook of action research: Participative inquiry and practice* (pp. 27–37). Thousand Oaks, CA: Sage.

Farrar, E., & House, E. (1986). The evaluation of PUSH/Excel: A case study. In E. R. House (Ed.), *New directions in educational evaluation* (pp. 158–185). London: Falmer Press.

Fecho, R. (1995). Words and lives: Toward a critical discourse on language among urban adolescents (Doctoral dissertation, University of Pennsylvania, 1995). *Dissertation Abstracts International, 57,* 136.

Fenstermacher, G. (1994). The knower and the known: The nature of knowledge in research on teaching. In L. Darling-Hammond (Ed.), *Review of Research in Education, 20,* 3–56.

Foshay, A. W. (1993). *Action research: An early history in the U.S.* Paper presented at the annual meeting of the American Educational Research Association, Atlanta, GA.

Foshay, A. W., & Wann, K. (1953). *Children's social values: An action research study.* New York: Bureau of Publications, Teachers College.

Foucault, M. (1980). *Power/Knowledge: Selected interviews and other writings, 1972–1977.* New York: Pantheon Books.

Fraser, N. (1996). *Justice interruptus: Critical reflections on the "postsocialist" condition.* New York: Routledge.

Freedman, S., Jackson, J., & Boles, K. (1986). *The effect of teaching on teachers.* Grand Forks: University of North Dakota Press.

Freire, P. (1970). *Pedagogy of the oppressed.* New York: Herder & Herder.

Fuller, R., & Petch, A. (1995). *Practitioner research: The reflexive social worker.* Buckingham, UK: Open University Press.

Gall, M., Gall, J., & Borg, W. (2003). *Educational research: An introduction* (7th ed.). Boston: Allyn and Bacon.

Gallas, K. (1993). *The languages of learning.* New York: Teachers College Press.

Gallas, K. (1997). *Sometimes I can be anything: Power, gender, and identity in a primary classroom.* New York: Teachers College Press.

Gallas, K. (2003). *Imagination and literacy: A teacher's search for the heart of learning.* New York: Teachers College Press.

Gaventa, J. (1988). Participatory research in North America: A perspective on participatory research in Latin America. *Convergence: An International Journal of Adult Education. 21*(2–3), 19–48.

Gaventa, J., & Horton, B. D. (1981). A citizen's research project in Appalachia, USA. *Convergence: An International Journal of Adult Education, 14*(3), 30–42.

Geertz, C. (1983). *Local knowledge: Further essays in interpretive anthropology.* New York: Basic Books.

Gibson, R. (1985). Critical times for action research. *Cambridge Journal of Education, 15*(1), 59–64.

Gitlin, A., Bringhurst, K., Burns, M., Cooley, V., Myers, B. Price, K., et al. (1992). *Teachers' voices for school change.* New York: Teachers College Press.

Glatthorm, A. (1998). *Writing the winning dissertation: A step-by-step guide.* Thousand Oaks, CA: Corwin.

Glickman, C. (1993). *Renewing America's schools: A guide for school-based action.* San Francisco: Jossey-Bass.

Goldin Rosenberg, D. (1999). Action for prevention: Feminist practices in transformative learning in women's health and the environment (with a focus on breast cancer). A case study of a participatory research circle. (Doctoral dissertation, University of Toronto, 1999). *Dissertation Abstracts International, 60,* 3587.

Gonzalez, J. L. (1991). Participatory action research: A view from FAGOR. In W. F. Whyte (Ed.), *Participatory action research* (pp. 77–84). Newbury Park, CA: Sage.

Goswami, D., & Stillman, P. R. (1987). *Reclaiming the classroom: Teacher research as an agency for change.* Upper Montclaire, NJ: Boynton.

Goswami, D., & Schultz, J. (1993). *Reclaiming the classroom: Teachers and students together.* Portsmouth, NH: Boynton/Cook.

Graves, D. (1981a). Research update: A new look at writing research. *Language Arts, 58*(2), 197–206.

Graves, D. (1981b). Research update: Where have all the teachers gone? *Language Arts, 58,* 492–497.

Greene, J. (1992). The practitioner's perspective. *Curriculum Inquiry, 22,* 39–45.

Greenwood, D., & Gonzalez, J. L. (Eds.). (1992). *Industrial democracy as process: Participatory action in the Fagor cooperative group of Mondragon.* Assen/Maastricht: Van Gorcum.

Greenwood, D., & Levin, M, (1998). *Introduction to action research: Social research for social change.* Thousand Oaks, CA: Sage.

Griffin, E., Lieberman, A., & Jacullo-Noto, J. (1982). *Interactive research and development of schooling: Final report.* New York: Teachers College.

Guba, E., & Lincoln, Y. (1989). *Fourth generation evaluation.* Thousand Oaks, CA: Sage.

Gustavsen, B. (1992). *Dialogue and development: Theory of communication.* Assen/Maastricht: Van Gorcum.

Habermas, J. (1971). *Knowledge and human interests.* Boston: Beacon Press.

Habermas, J. (1979). *Communication and the evolution of society.* Boston: Beacon Press.

Hall, B. (2001). I wish this were a poem of practices of participatory research. In P. Reason & H. Bradbury (Eds.), *Handbook of action research: Participative inquiry and practice* (pp. 171–178). Thousand Oaks, CA: Sage.

Hall, S. (1996). Reflexivity in emancipatory action research: Illustrating the researcher's consitutiveness. In O. Zuber-Skerritt (Ed.), *New directions in action research* (pp. 28–48). London: Falmer Press.

Hammack, F. M. (1997). Ethical issues in teacher research. *Teachers College Record, 99*(2), 247–265.

Hart, C. (1998). Doing a literature review: Releasing the social science research imagination. Thousand Oaks, CA: Sage.

Harwood, D. (1991). Action research vs. interaction analysis: A time for reconciliation? A reply to Barry Hutchinson. *British Educational Research Journal, 17,* 67–72.

Headman, R. R. (1992). Parents' perspectives on children's literacy: A parent/teacher co-investigation (Doctoral dissertation, University of Pennsylvania, 1992). *Dissertation Abstracts International, 53,* 3857.

Hepner, P., & Hepner, M. (2003). *Writing and publishing your thesis, dissertation, and research: A guide for students in the helping professions.* Belmont, CA: Wadsworth.

Heron, J. (1996). *Co-operative inquiry: Research into the human condition.* London: Sage.

Herr, K. (1995). Action research as empowering practice. *Journal of Progressive Human Services, 6*(2), 45–58.

Herr, K. (1999a). The symbolic uses of participation: Co-opting change. *Theory Into Practice, 38*(4), 235–240.

Herr, K. (1999b). Unearthing the unspeakable: When teacher research and political agendas collide. *Language Arts, 77*(1), 10–15.

Herr, K. (1999c). Private power and privileged education: De/constructing institutionalized racism. *Journal of Inclusive Education, 3*(2), 111–129.

Herr, K. (1999d). Institutional violence in the everyday practices of school: The narrative of a young lesbian. *Journal for a Just and Caring Education, 5*(3), 242–255.

Holly, P. (1989). Action research: Cul-de-sac or turnpike? *Peabody Journal of Education, 64*(3), 71–100.

Holmes Group. (1990). *Tomorrow's schools: Principles for the design of professional development schools.* East Lansing, MI: The Holmes Group.

Hoonaard, W. C., van den (2001). Is research-ethics review a moral panic? *The Canadian Review of Sociology and Anthropology, 38*(1), 19–36.

Howe, K. R., & Moses, M. (1999). Ethics in educational research. In A. Iran-Nejad & P. D. Pearson (Eds.), *Review of research in education* (pp. 21–59). Washington, DC: AERA.

Hubbard, R., & Power, B. M. (1999). *Living the questions: A guide for teacher-researchers.* York, ME: Stenhouse.

Huberman, M. (1996). Focus on research moving mainstream: Taking a closer look at teacher research. *Language Arts, 73*(2), 124–140.

Israel, B., Schultz, A., Parker, E., Becker, A., Allen, A., & Guzman, J. R. (2003). Critical issues in developing and following community based participatory principals. In M. Minkler & N. Wallerstein (Eds.), *Community-based participatory research for health* (pp. 53–76). San Francisco: Jossey-Bass.

Jacobson, W. (1998). Defining the quality of practitioner research. *Adult Education Quarterly, 48*(3), 125–139.

Jason, L., Keys, C., Balcazar, Y., Taylor, R., Davis, M., Durlak, J., et al. (Eds.). (2003). *Participatory community research: Theories and methods in action.* Washington, DC: American Psychological Association.

Johnson, R. S. (2002). *Using data to close the achievement gap: How to measure equity in our schools.* Thousand Oaks, CA: Corwin.

Kelly, J. G. (1999). Contexts and community leadership: Inquiry as an ecological expedition. *American Psychologist, 54,* 953–961.

Kelly, J. G., Azelton, S., Lardon, C., Mock, L. O., Tandon, D., & Thomas, M. (2004). On community leadership: Stories about collaboration in action research. *American Journal of Community Psychology, 33,* 205–216.

Kelly, J. G., Mock, L., & Tandon, S. D. (2001). Collaborative inquiry with African-American community leaders: Comments on a participatory research process. In P. Reason & H. Bradbury (Eds.), *Handbook of action research: Participative inquiry & practice* (pp. 348–355). London: Sage.

Kemmis, S. (Ed.). (1982). *The action research reader.* Geelong, Victoria, Australia: Deakin University Press.

Kemmis, S. (2001). Exploring the relevance of critical theory for action research: Emancipatory action research in the footsteps of Jurgen Habermas. In P. Reason & H. Bradbury, *Handbook of action research: Participative inquiry and practice* (pp. 91–102). Thousand Oaks, CA: Sage.

Kemmis, S., & McTaggart, R. (1987). *The action research planner.* Geelong, Victoria, Australia: Deakin University Press.

Kincheloe, J. L. (1991). *Teachers as researchers: Qualitative inquiry as a path to empowerment.* Philadelphia: Falmer Press.

Kingry-Westergaard, C., & Kelly, J. G. (1986). A contextualist epistemology for ecological research. In P. Tolan, C. Keys, F. Chertok, & L. Jason (Eds.), *Researching community psychology: Issues of theory and methods* (pp. 23–31). Washington, DC: American Psychological Association.

Knight, M. G. (2000). Ethics in qualitative research: Multicultural feminist activist research. *Theory Into Practice, 39*(3), 170–176.

Lather, P. (1986a). Issues of validity in openly ideological research: Between a rock and a hard place. *Interchange, 17,* 63–84.

Lather, P. (1986b). Research as praxis. *Harvard Educational Review, 56*(3), 257–277.

LeCompte, M., & Schensul, J. J. (1999). *Designing and conducting ethnographic research.* Walnut Creek, CA: Alta Mira Press.

Lee, C., Smagorinsky, P., Pea, R., Brown, J. S., & Heath, C. (1999). *Vygotskian perspectives on literacy research: Constructing meaning through collaborative inquiry.* Cambridge, UK: University of Cambridge Press.

Levin, M. (1999). Action research paradigms. In D. Greenwood (Ed.), *Action research: From practice to writing in an international action research development program* (pp. 25–37). Amsterdam: John Benjamins.

Lewin, K. (1946). Action research and minority problems. *Journal of Social Issues, 2*(4), 34–46.

Lewin, K. (1948). *Resolving social conflicts.* New York: Harper and Rowe.

Lewis, H. (2001). Participatory research and education for social change: Highlander research and education center. In P. Reason & H. Bradbury (Eds.), *Handbook of action research: Participative inquiry and practice* (pp. 356–362). Thousand Oaks, CA: Sage.

Lieberman, A., & Miller, L. (1984). School improvement: Themes and variations. *Teachers College Record, 86,* 4–19.

Lincoln, Y., & Guba, E. (1985). *Naturalistic inquiry.* Beverly Hills, CA: Sage.

Lindblom, C., & Cohen, D. (1979). *Usable knowledge: Social science and social problem solving.* New Haven, CT: Yale University Press.

Lindblom, C. (1995). *Inquiry and change: The troubled attempt to understand and shape society.* New Haven, CT: Yale University Press.

Liston, D. P., & Zeichner, K. M. (1991). *Teacher education and the social conditions of schooling.* New York: Routledge.

Lomax, P., Woodward, C., & Parker, Z. (1996). How can we help educational managers establish and implement effective 'critical' friendships? In P. Lomax (Ed.), *Quality management in education: Sustaining the vision through action research* (pp. 152–165). London: Routledge.

Luft, J. (1963). *Group process: An introduction to group dynamics.* Palo Alto, CA: National Press Books.

Maguire, P. (1987a). Developing a framework for feminist participatory research: A case and assessment with former battered women in Gallup, New Mexico (Doctoral dissertation, University of Massachusetts, 1987). *Dissertation Abstracts International, 48,* 357.

Maguire, P. (1987b). *Doing participatory research: A feminist approach.* Amherst: Center for International Education, University of Massachusetts.

Maguire, P. (1993). Challenges, contradictions, and celebrations: Attempting participatory research as a doctoral student. In P. Park, M. Brydon-Miller, B. Hall, & T. Jackson (Eds.), *Voices of change: Participatory research in the United States and Canada* (pp. 157–176). Westport, CT: Bergin & Garvey.

Martin, N. (1987). On the move: Teacher researchers. In D. Goswami & P. Stillman (Eds.), *Reclaiming the classroom: Teacher research as an agency for change* (pp. 20–28). Upper Montclaire, NJ: Boynton/Cook.

Martin R. (1998). What do we mean when we say co-learner? Reconsidering Freirian pedagogy: New methods for radical adult literacy (Doctoral dissertation, University of New Mexico, 1998). *Dissertation Abstracts International, 59,* 4093.

Martin, R. (2001). *Listening up: Reinventing ourselves as teachers and students.* Portsmouth, NH: Heinemann.

Mastroianni, A., & Kahn, J. (2001). Swinging on the pendulum: Shifting views of justice in human subjects research. *Hastings Center Report, 31*(3), 21–28.

McCarthy, C. R. (1998). The institutional review board: Its origins, purposes, function and future. In D. N. Weisstub (Ed.), *Research on human subjects: Ethics, law and social policy* (pp. 286–300). Oxford, UK: Pergamon Press.

McCutcheon, G., & Jung, B. (1990). Alternative perspectives on action research. *Theory Into Practice, 29*(3), 144–151.

McIntyre, A. (1995). Making meaning of whiteness: Participatory action research with white female student teachers (Doctoral dissertation, Boston College, 1995). *Dissertation Abstracts International, 57,* 175.

McIntyre, A. (1997a). *Making meaning of whiteness: Exploring racial identity with white teachers.* Albany, NY: SUNY Press.

McIntyre, A. (1997b). Constructing an image of a white teacher. *Teachers College Record, 98*(4), 653–681.

McKernan, J. (1988). The countenance of curriculum action research: Traditional, collaborative, and emancipatory-critical conceptions. *Journal of Curriculum and Supervision, 3*(3), 173–200.

McLaughlin, T. (1996). *Street smarts and critical theory: Listening to the vernacular.* Madison: University of Wisconsin Press.

McLeod, J. (1999). *Practitioner research in counseling.* Thousand Oaks, CA: Corwin.

McNeil, L. (2000). *Contradictions of school reform: The educational costs of standardized testing.* New York: Routledge.

McNiff, J., & Whitehead, J. (2000). *Action research in organisations.* New York: Routledge.

Meloy, J. M. (2001). *Writing the qualitative dissertation: Understanding by doing* (2nd ed.). Mahwah, NJ: Lawrence Erlbaum.

Miller, J. (1990). *Creating spaces and finding voices: Teachers collaborating for empowerment.* Albany: State University of New York Press.

Mills, G. E. (2002). *Action research: A guide for the teacher researcher.* Columbus, OH: Merrill.

Minkler, M., & Wallerstein, N. (Eds.). (2002). *Community-based participatory research for health.* San Francisco: Jossey-Bass.

Mishler, E. G. (1986). *Research interviewing: Context and narrative.* Cambridge, MA: Harvard University Press.

Mock, L. O. (1999). The personal visions of African-American community leaders (Doctoral dissertation, University of Illinois at Chicago, 1999). *Dissertation Abstracts International, 60,* 6424.

Moller, J. (1998). Action research with principals: Gain, strain and dilemmas. *Educational Action Research, 6*(1), 69–91.

Morton-Cooper, A. (2000). *Action research in health care.* London: Blackwell.

Myers, M. (1985). *The teacher-researcher: How to study writing in the classroom.* Urbana, IL: National Council of Teachers of English.

National Commission for the Protection of Human Subjects of Biomedical and Behavioral Research. (1979). *The Belmont report: Ethical principles and guidelines for the protection of human subjects of research.* Retrieved February 25, 2004 from http://ohsr.od.nih.gov/mpa/belmont.php3

Noffke, S. (1990). Action research: A multidimensional analysis (Doctoral dissertation, University of Wisconsin, 1990). *Dissertation Abstracts International, 51,* 2973.

Noffke, S., & Brennan, M. (1991). Action research and reflective student teaching at the University of Wisconsin-Madison: Issues and examples. In B. R. Tabachnik & K. Zeichner (Eds.), *Issues and practices in inquiry-oriented teacher education* (pp. 186–201). London: Falmer Press.

O'Donnell-Allen, C. L. (1999). Teaching with a questioning mind: An analysis of the development of a teacher research group into a discourse community (Doctoral dissertation, University of Oklahoma, 1990). *Dissertation Abstracts International, 60*, 3970.

Oja, S., & Ham, M. (1984). A cognitive-developmental approach to collaborative action research with teachers. *Teachers College Record, 86*, 171–192.

Palshaugen, O. (1998). *The end of organization theory? Language as a tool in action research.* Amsterdam: John Benjamins.

Patton, M. (1996). *Utilization-focused evaluation* (3rd ed.). Thousand Oaks, CA: Sage.

Patton, M. (2001). *Qualitative research and evaluation methods.* Thousand Oaks, CA: Sage.

Pelletier, B. (2001). Management practices, soil quality and maize yield in smallholder farming systems of central Malawi (Doctoral dissertation, McGill University, 2001). *Dissertation Abstracts International, 63*, 3075.

Perez, E. (2000). Empowerment in Pacora, Nicaragua: Use of local knowledge and participatory action research to promote sustainable agriculture and natural resources management (Doctoral dissertation, Cornell University, 2000). *Dissertation Abstracts International, 61*, 2293.

Piantanida, M., & Garman, N. (1999). *The qualitative dissertation: A guide for students and faculty.* Thousand Oaks, CA: Corwin.

Polanyi, M. (1958). *Personal knowledge.* Chicago: University of Chicago Press.

Pritchard, I. (2002). Travelers and trolls: Practitioner research and institutional review boards. *Educational Researcher, 31*(3), 3–13.

Reason, P. (1994). Three approaches to participatory inquiry. In N. Denzin & Y. Lincoln (Eds.), *Handbook of qualitative research* (pp. 324–339). Thousand Oaks, CA: Sage.

Reason, P., & Bradbury, H. (Eds.). (2001a). *Handbook of action research: Participative inquiry and practice.* Thousand Oaks, CA: Sage.

Reason, P., & Bradbury, H. (2001b). Preface. In P. Reason & H. Bradbury (Eds.), *Handbook of action research: Participative inquiry and practice* (pp. xxiii–xxxi). Thousand Oaks, CA: Sage.

Reason, P., & Marshall, J. (2001). On working with graduate research students. In P. Reason & H. Bradbury (Eds.), *Handbook of action research: Participative inquiry and practice* (pp. 413–419). Thousand Oaks, CA: Sage.

Reed-Danahay, D. (Ed.). (1997). *Auto/ethnography: Rewriting the self and the social.* New York: Berg.

Richardson, V. (1994). Conducting research on practice. *Educational Researcher, 23*(5), 5–10.

Rivera, M. (1999). *The spirit of resistance: A participatory action research project with six Puerto Rican and Dominican young women.* (Doctoral dissertation, Harvard University). *Dissertation Abstracts International, 60*, 3020.

Robinson, V. (1993). *Problem-based methodology: Research for the improvement of practice.* Oxford, UK: Pergamon Press.

Rogoff, B, Turkanis, C. G., & Bartlett, L. (2001). *Learning together: Children and adults in a school community.* Oxford, UK: Oxford University Press.

Roman, L. (1992). The political significance of other ways of narrating ethnography: A feminist materialist approach. In M. LeCompte, W. Millroy, & J. Preissle (Eds.), *The handbook of qualitative research in education* (pp. 555–592). San Diego, CA: Academic Press.

Rudestam, K., & Newton, R. (1992). *Surviving your dissertation: A comprehensive guide to content and process.* Newbury Park, CA: Sage.

Saavedra, E. (1994). *Teacher transformation: Creating texts and contexts in study groups.* Unpublished doctoral dissertation, University of Arizona, Tucson, AZ.

Saavedra, E. (1996). Teacher study groups: Contexts for transformative learning and action. *Theory Into Practice, 35*(4), 271–277.

Sanders, D., & McCutcheon, G. (1986). The development of practical theories of teaching. *Journal of Curriculum and Supervision. 2*(1), 50–67.

Sanford, N. (1970). Whatever happened to action research? *Journal of Social Issues, 26,* 3–23.

Schaefer, R. J. (1967). *The school as a center of inquiry.* New York: Harper and Row.

Schon, D. (1983). *The reflective practitioner: How professionals think in action.* New York: Basic Books.

Schon, D. (1987). *Educating the reflective practitioner.* San Francisco: Jossey-Bass.

Schubert, W., & Lopez-Schubert, A. (1997). Sources of a theory for action research in the United States of America. In R. McTaggart (Ed.), *Participatory action research: International contexts and consequences* (pp. 203–222). Albany, NY: SUNY Press.

Schwartz, T. A. (2002). 'Write me': A participatory action research project with urban Appalachian girls (Doctoral dissertation, University of Cincinnati, 2002). *Dissertation Abstracts International, 63,* 1695.

Scott, J. C. (1990). *Domination and the arts of resistance: Hidden transcripts.* New Haven, CT: Yale University Press.

Seigart, D. M. (1999). Participatory evaluation and community learning: Sharing knowledge about school-based health care (Doctoral dissertation, Cornell University, 2002). *Dissertation Abstracts International, 60,* 901.

Sirotnik, K. (1988). The meaning and conduct of inquiry in school-university partnerships. In K. Sirotnik & J. Goodlad (Eds.), *School-university partnerships in action.* New York: Teachers College Press.

Smith-Maddox, R. (1999). An inquiry-based reform effort: Creating the conditions for reculturing and restructuring schools. *Urban Review, 31*(3), 283–304.

Spjelkavik, O. (1999). Applied research or action research? Different or complementary methods. In D. Greenwood (Ed.), *Action research: From practice to writing in an international action research development program* (pp. 117–130). Amsterdam: John Benjamins.

Stake, R. (Ed.). (1975). *Evaluating the arts in education: A responsive approach.* Columbus, OH: Merrill.

Stake, R. (1986). An evolutionary view of educational improvement. In E. R. House (Ed.), *New directions in educational evaluation* (pp. 89–102). London: Falmer Press.

Stanton-Salazar, R. (2001). *Manufacturing hope and despair: The school and kin support networks of U.S.-Mexican youth.* New York: Teachers College Press.

Stringer, E., & Genat, W. (2004). *Action research in health.* New York: Prentice Hall.

Tandon, S. D., Kelly, J. G., & Mock, L. (2001). Participatory action research as a resource for developing African American community leadership. In D. Tolman and M. Brydon-Miller (Eds.), *From subjects to subjectivities: A handbook of interpretive and participatory methods* (pp. 200–217). New York: New York University Press.

Tanke, E. D. & Tanke, T. J. (1982). Regulation and education: The role of the institutional review board in social sciences research. In J. E. Sieber (Ed.), *The ethics of social research: fieldwork, regulation and publication* (pp. 131–149). New York: Springer-Verlag.

Tenni, C., Smyth, A., & Boucher, C. (2003). The researcher as autobiographer: Analysing data written about oneself [Electronic version]. *The Qualitative Report, 8*(1). Retrieved November 23, 2003 from www.nova.edu/ssss/QR/QR8–1/tenni.html

Tikunoff, J., Ward, B., & Griffin, G. (1979). *Interactive research and development on teaching study: Final report.* San Francisco: Far West Laboratory for Educational Research and Development.

Tisdale, K. (2003). Being vulnerable: Being ethical with/in research. In K. deMarrais & S. Lapan (Eds.), *Foundations for research: Methods of inquiry in education and social sciences* (pp. 13–30). Mahwah, NJ: Lawrence Erlbaum.

Tolley, E., & Bentley, M. (1996). Training issues for the use of participatory research methods in health. In K. De Koning & M. Martin (Eds.), *Participatory research in health: Issues and experience* (pp. 50–61). London: Zed Books.

Tolman, D., & Brydon-Miller, M. (2001). Interpretive and participatory research methods: Moving toward subjectivities. In D. Tolman & M. Brydon-Miller (Eds.), *From subjects to subjectivities: A handbook of interpretive and participatory methods* (pp. 3–11). New York: New York University Press.

Toness, A. S. (2002). Assessment of participatory rural appraisal (PRA): The effects of practicing PRA among development institutions and rural communities in Paraguay (Doctoral dissertation, Texas A & M University, 2002). *Dissertation Abstracts International, 63,* 2771.

Torbert, W. (1981). Why educational research has been so uneducational: The case for a new model of social science based on collaborative inquiry. In P. Reason & J. Rowan (Eds.), *Human inquiry: A sourcebook of new paradigm research* (pp. 141–151). New York: John Wiley.

Tripp, D. (1990). Socially critical action research. *Theory Into Practice, 24*(3), 158–166.

Tripp, D. (1994). *Critical incidents in teaching: Developing professional judgement.* London: Routledge.

Tuhiwai Smith, L. (1999). *Decolonizing methodologies: Research and indigenous peoples.* London: Zed Books.

Tuttle, S. L. (2003). Gender roles and participatory delivery strategies for selected villagers in northeastern Mexico (Doctoral dissertation, Texas A & M University, 2003). *Dissertation Abstracts International, 64,* 1158.

van Beinum, H. (1999). On the design of the ACRES program. In D. Greenwood (Ed.), *Action research: From practice to writing in an international action research development program* (pp. 3–24). Amsterdam: John Benjamins.

Villenas, S. (1996). The colonizer/colonized Chicana ethnographer: Identity, marginalization, and co-optation in the field. *Harvard Educational Review, 66*(4), 711–731.

Wallerstein, N., & Duran, B. (2003). The conceptual, historical, and practice roots of community based participatory research and related participatory traditions. In M. Minkler & N. Wallerstein (Eds.), *Community-based participatory research for health* (pp. 27–54). San Francisco: Jossey-Bass.

Watkins, K. (1991, April). *Validity in action research.* Paper presented at the annual meeting of the American Educational Research Association, Chicago. (ED 334 246).

Wax, M. L. (1982). Research reciprocity rather than informed consent in fieldwork. In J. E. Sieber (Ed.), *The ethics of social research: Fieldwork, regulation, and publication.* New York: Springer-Verlag.

Webb, G. (1996). Becoming critical of action research for development. In O. Zuber-Skerritt (Ed.), *New directions in action research* (pp. 137–161). London: Falmer Press.

Weiner, G. (1989). Professional self-knowledge versus social justice: A critical analysis of the teacher-researcher movement. *British Educational Research Journal, 15*, 41–51.

Weiss, C. (1987). Where politics and evaluation research meet. In D. J. Palumbo (Ed.), *The politics of program evaluation* (pp. 47–70). Newbury Park, CA: Sage.

Whitford, B. L., Schlechty, P. C., & Shelor, L. G. (1989). Sustaining action research through collaboration: Inquiries for invention. *Peabody Journal of Education, 64*(3), 151–169.

Whitehead, J. (1989). Creating a living educational theory from questions of the kind: How do I improve my practice? *Cambridge Journal of Education, 19*, 41–52.

Whitehead, J., & Lomax, P. (1987). Action research and the politics of educational knowledge. *British Educational Research Journal, 13*(2), 175–190.

Whyte, J. B. (1987). Issues and dilemmas in action research. In G. Wolford (Ed.), *Doing sociology of education.* Philadelphia: Falmer Press.

Whyte, W. F. (1991). Conclusions. In W. F. Whyte (Ed.), *Participatory action research* (pp. 237–241). Newbury Park, CA: Sage.

Willinsky, J. (2000). *Learning to divide the world: Education at Empire's end.* Minneapolis: University of Minnesota Press.

Winter, R. (1989). *Learning from experience: Principles and practice in action research.* Lewes, Sussex, UK: Falmer Press.

Wong, D. E. (1995a). Challenges confronting the researcher/teacher: Conflicts of purpose and conduct. *Educational Researcher, 24*(3), 22–28.

Wong, D. E. (1995b). Challenges confronting the researcher/teacher: A rejoinder to Wilson. *Educational Researcher, 24*(8), 22–23.

Yopo, B. (1984). *Metodologia de la investigacion participativa* [A methodology for participatory research]. Patzcuaro, Michoacan, Mexico: Cuadernos del CREFAL.

Zeichner, K. (1981–1982). Reflective teaching and field based experience in teacher education. *Interchange, 12*(4), 1–22.

Zeichner, K., & Noffke, S. (2002). Practitioner research. In V. Richardson (Ed.), *Handbook of research on teaching* (4th ed.). Washington, DC: American Educational Research Association.

Zeni, J. (2001). A guide to ethical decision making for insider research. In J. Zeni (Ed.), *Ethical issues in practitioner research* (pp. 153–165). New York: Teachers College Press.

Zuniga-Urrutia, X. (1992). Views and issues in action research (research methods) (Doctoral dissertation, University of Michigan, 1992). *Dissertation Abstracts International, 53*, 3459.

Index

About the Authors

Kathryn Herr is a faculty member in the College of Education and Human Services at Montclair State University in Montclair, New Jersey. She is coauthor of the book *Studying Your Own School: An Educator's Guide to Qualitative Practitioner Research* (1994, Thousand Oaks, CA: Corwin Press). She is also editor of the interdisciplinary journal *Youth and Society*. Her professional background is in social work and education.

Gary L. Anderson is a faculty member in the Department of Administration, Leadership, and Technology in the Steinhardt School of Education, New York University. He is a former teacher and high school principal. He has written numerous articles on action research, including (with Kathryn Herr) "The new paradigm wars. Is there room for rigorous practitioner knowledge in schools and universities?" (1999, *Educational Researcher, 28*[5], 12–21). In recent publications, he has explored applications of critical and postmodern theory and critical discourse analysis to the field of educational leadership.